# Language Comprehension Success with Shared Strategic Reading

*Features the Original Story:*

***Guff's Journey***

David Newman

Speech-language Pathologist

SpeechLanguage-Resources

User-Friendly Games and Activities

A Friendly Reminder



ISBN-13: 978-1492912705

*To the hard-working speech-language pathologists and all Student Support Services staff, whose commitment to provide great service to schools helps to make such a positive difference to peoples' lives*

# Language Comprehension Success with Shared Strategic Reading

David Newman

www.speechlanguage-resources.com

# Preface

## Audience

During my 15 years as a school-based speech language clinician, I have used any number of techniques and activities to engage students with text and storybooks. In my experience, students' ability to comprehend what they read is intimately tied to their knowledge and use of oral language. The intention of this manual is for speech-language clinicians, teachers, and teacher aides to use various exercises and techniques to help improve students' language comprehension and their ability to engage with and comprehend text.

## Background

This workbook began several years ago. Back then I became frustrated using what I would call traditional language intervention. I always felt that there was a gap between the oral language skills I attempted to teach students and the skills they needed to read and comprehend age appropriate text. Though effective in many ways, traditional language intervention methods focus on teaching discrete language skills, mostly in isolation and not tied to a particular context. I was looking for something new. On a literature search I discovered a form of language intervention with high efficacy known as contextualized language intervention, which also goes by the title shared reading or shared strategic reading. Contextualized language intervention emphasizes the use of meaningful fiction and non-fiction text to facilitate students' understanding and use of complex oral and written language forms.

## Organisation

The language comprehension workbook has 12 chapters. The introduction explains some of the theory of shared reading strategies. Chapter 2 features the Guff's Journey story which is the basis for assessment and intervention of all the chapters to follow. Chapter 3 explores ways of using the Guff's Journey text as a means of informal assessment of students' reading and reading comprehension skills. In chapter 4 the emphasis is auditory recall of literal and inferred details from the text. Chapter 5 focuses on developing syntax and grammar skills, again using the context of the story to explore complex language. In both chapters 6 and 7 the emphasis is on key comprehension skills: problem solving and inference skills. Students are prompted to imagine what it might be like to be Guff or his sister Asa in the prehistoric world. All previous chapters are solid preparation for chapters 9-10, which feature techniques and examples of shared strategic reading strategies and how best to utilise them. Chapter 11 focuses on how to use pictograms to facilitate story grammar knowledge. The appendices feature several other activities worth exploring, an answer key and a variety of high utility graphic organizers and record forms.

**David Newman**

# Contents

# 1

# *Introduction:*

# Understanding Language Comprehension

The activities featured in the Language Comprehension Success workbook are focused on an original short story, *Guff's Journey*. The story comes complete with a series of tasks and questions, to be completed by students. Hand drawn illustrations are a feature of the story and provide a visual aid and further context for students. *Guff's Journey* is about a Neanderthal boy separated from his tribe. Guff faces the dangers of the prehistoric world alone as he attempts to find a way back to his people.

### Shared Strategic Reading

Shared strategic reading is a literature based language intervention that has strong efficacy in helping children overcome oral and written language comprehension difficulty. Literature based intervention is an effective way to teach students language and reading comprehension skills. Speech-language pathologists who use this method do not specifically teach decoding skills; instead, the focus is on unlocking and parsing the oral and written language that underpins literacy. Shared strategic reading works by parsing written text – stories and picture books - to teach language comprehension skills. Learning abstract language concepts within a familiar context helps to lessen the problems associated with decon-textualized language. Shared strategic reading's primary goal is for a clinician to use a storybook as a therapeutic tool to improve students' language knowledge and comprehension. Text and illustrations become the primary source of language stimulation, which is expertly shaped and scaffolded by the clinician. The story is parsed and broken down in detail using the text and pictures in a systematic way. The result is that clinicians prompt students to think about literacy and language in a unique way. Shared strategic reading helps to support students' comprehension of stories and academic text with the ultimate aim of producing independent readers who habitually read for meaning. Chapter 10 features excellent examples of shared strategic reading and demonstrates how to parse and dissect key story themes and language.

### Metalinguistic Awareness

A key target of language comprehension intervention is to improve students' metalinguistic awareness. Meta-linguistics or meta-awareness skill is the ability of a person to reflect on and consciously ponder about oral and written language. Meta is an ancient Greek term, meaning beyond. In the context of language learning, meta means going beyond overt communication and meaning to focus attention on the underlying language structures. Successful language and reading comprehension is centered on the student being aware of language and the components of language. Meta- awareness skill is at work when a student is able to switch attention from the content of what they or others say to the saying itself. This ability - metalinguistic awareness - is a vital skill in language comprehension.

## Reading Comprehension

Comprehension of text is perhaps the most important aspect of reading and is dependent on language comprehension skills. Successful reading comprehension is far more than just recognizing and decoding words on a page, and more than simply comprehending individual words. For true understanding of text, readers have to integrate their phonetic knowledge of word and syntactical structures with their semantic word knowledge, essentially word and world knowledge. Readers with cognitive or language difficulties often find comprehension of written material challenging due to difficulty going beyond surface details in text to infer meaning. Language and reading comprehension failure is complex and can occur for a number of different reasons. For students to comprehend an author's message, it requires them to analyse and mentally sort through multiple layers of text meaning. Four main areas contribute to language and reading comprehension success.

1. To successfully comprehend a written passage, a student must first be able to decode the text.

2. The student needs to be able retain the information in working memory long enough for the information to be manipulated mentally and processed efficiently.

3. The student requires adequate vocabulary, grammar and syntactical skills to organize and interpret the written information efficiently.

4. The student then needs to access higher order thinking skills to process the written information and go beyond surface details to infer deeper meaning.

## Comprehension and Context

The term context relates to the parts directly before and after a word that influences its meaning. When readers encounter a new and unfamiliar word, the best method of determining a word's meaning is to note how the words and sentences that are positioned before and after the target word relate to it. For instance, if we encounter the word *cumulus* without context we may have difficulty understanding the word's meaning. However, we may place the word *cumulus* in a passage such as, *the cumulus drifted in the upper atmosphere concealing the sun.* Within the context of the above sentence, *cumulus* refers to a type of cloud. A reader with poor comprehension skills may still have difficulty understanding the sentences meaning if their understanding of the term upper atmosphere is poor. Context can be problematic for students with poor vocabularies and reduced semantic word knowledge. In this situation, a teacher would need to provide scaffolding such as shared strategic reading and graphic organizers to provide a foundation of knowledge of weather and cloud formations to assist students' understanding of the word *cumulus*.

## Comprehension and Inference

Children with poor reading comprehension skills have difficulty with inference mostly because of their difficulty in plunging beneath the surface level of text. To infer what is happening in a story is a vital higher order thinking skill. Inference skill enables readers to interpret and surmise what an author may only hint at. Inference requires a close reading and understanding of the text and is a vital skill for all reading and language comprehension, both fiction and non-fiction.

## Available as a free download

**Important note:** The materials in the *Language Comprehension Success* book are best used by photocopying the pages and completing the exercises on the page itself. Unfortunately the book is only available in perfect bound, which can be difficult to photocopy. With this in mind, I have created a webpage where all the individual chapters and appendices can be **downloaded** and **printed.**

The webpage is…
http://www.speechlanguage-resources.com/journey-home-program.html

Write the above code into your website browser. Specific instructions for this can be found on page 219.

# 2

## *Story:*

## Guff's Journey

# Guff's Journey

The Guff's Journey story was developed and written specifically for this workbook. Guff's Journey is an original story that has many of the features and complexity of commercially available story books. The text has been written for children between the ages of 9 -12 years of age. Younger readers can also read and enjoy the story, though some of the story's themes may need to be scaffolded due to complexity. The Fleisch Kincaid (available on Word 2007, 2010 and 2013) places the story's complexity in terms of sentence length and complexity of language as approximately grade 4.

The story has a simple, linear plot and features several key characters, such as the main protagonist Guff, and Guff's father, Utha. The story also boasts a mighty bull mammoth known as a muloth by the Neanderthal people in the context of the story, and a truly frightening saber-toothed cat. We gain insight into Guff's world through his observations, sensations and experiences of the harsh prehistoric world that he and his tribe are a part of.

The story is written in a style which is relatively easy to use as a language teaching tool. The language in the story is complex at times and figurative language is used to provide colour to dramatic scenes. Illustrations are utilized to provide a visual reference to the story's setting - the wilderness of prehistoric earth, somewhere in modern day Europe. Students are encouraged to read the story independently. Alternatively, Guff's Journey can be read by both the clinician and the student together. The Guff's Journey story is used as the example text for each chapter in this workbook.

**Story:** *Guff's Journey* - Words and illustrations by David Newman

**Description:** Guff is a Neanderthal boy who, due to a hunting misadventure, becomes separated from his tribe. Guff relies on his wits, courage and ability to adapt in order to survive in a harsh environment. Guff is resourceful and is a good problem solver.

**Reading Age:** 9 – 12 years

**Fleisch Kincaid Level:** Grade 3.3

**Total Words:** 2077

## Instructions for Reading and Reading Comprehension Assessment based on Guff's Journey

The student is required to read a passage of the text or the entire text, depending on the student's level of reading competency. For readers who struggle with the text's complexity, it is recommended that only one scene be completed at a time. Each scene is long enough and contains enough information to obtain both a reading error analysis and reading comprehension analysis. Multiple examples of reading and reading comprehension analysis are provided in chapter 3.

## Instructions for Shared Reading of the Entire Guff's Journey Story

Read the story aloud with the student, with either you or the student reading, or a combination of the two. Pause at different points in the story to comment on important plot developments, character motivations, or interesting language. Review chapters 8 and 9 for tips and strategies on how to engage students with the Guff's Journey text.

## Scene 1

The dry grass pressed fierce into Guff's legs as he lay in the dirt, but he did not complain. Guff was on his first hunt with the elders and he needed to be quiet as a field mouse. Above the hunters loomed a mighty bull muloth, its tusks curved and lethal. Sweat beaded Guff's forehead though the day was cold. Guff's father, Utha, anxious for Guff, searched Guff's eyes and then smiled. Utha's arm muscles were tense and corded as if carved from oak. He lay flat beside other men of the tribe a short spear toss from Guff. Between the tribe's spears and fat calves was the bull.

Guff's heart flipped like a fish when the bull suddenly stomped close to where he lay. The brute had located a rich cluster of long grass that unhappily was just above Guff's head. The snort of the giant's breath rippled Guff's hair, while the stink of its shaggy mane filled his nostrils. The muloth tore out chunks of grass and crushed it in its jaws. Another mouthful and Guff's cover would be gone. Guff's hands trembled as he gripped his stone-tipped spear. He could not breathe well. This was happening too fast. His heart thumped like a leather drum beaten with a stick. The pounding was so loud in Guff's ears that he was certain the bull would hear.

## Scene 2

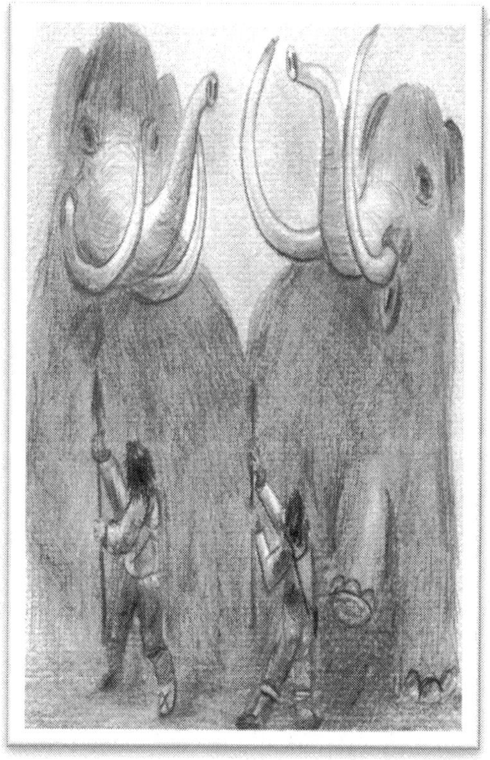

What happened next were swift, fleeting actions and blasts of noise - men shouting and the furious peal and roar of the muloths. Spears buzzed through the air like insects. Guff stood though had no memory of getting to his feet. Something big hit him in the side and he soared through the air, weightless. The next instant the air was ripped from his chest when he struck the hard dirt. The big sky whirled. He could hear Utha above the confusion, howling, 'Guff, Guff'. He tried to call to his father but his mouth failed to form the words.

Guff scrambled to his feet as blood surged to his head. His thoughts were jumbled, so he ran. His father and tribe were gone, scattered. Guff sensed something enormous shadow him. He felt the rhythmic crunch of its hooves impact the ground just behind him, its breath a series of loud bursts. Soon it would crush him. Guff's chest was a torment from fatigue as he strained to keep running. In his panic, Guff failed to see that the ground had suddenly vanished from under him. He shrieked and fell into blackness down a steep hill.

Much later, Guff slowly opened his eyes and winced. Sunlight trickled in. His thoughts were murky. He could make out shadows and shapes and saw that the sun was about to leave the big sky. The muloth was gone. The half-light before dark crept with long fingers across the land. Guff's fogginess cleared. He saw for the first time that he lay in a ditch. His back ached but he could move his limbs. His spear lay beside him, undamaged. Guff's stone blade, wrapped in its leather pouch, was still attached to his leggings. His father would be pleased. He slowly poked his head above the ditch. He was in a deep ravine. Mountains rose sharp and pitiless on all sides. In the half-light, the peaks were cold, vast and glowing. The last wisps of gold and warmth clung to the tops of the harsh crests. Too soon, the threads of light faded to nothing and the evening gloom deepened. Guff was alone in the dark for the first time in his life.

**Scene 3**

Guff huddled and shivered beneath the great night orb. His father's words bounced in his head. "If lost at night. Make no sound. Be not seen nor heard." Guff was indeed lost. The search for his tribe would begin with first light, but first he had to survive the night. Guff wrapped himself in his furs but the cold defeated him. He stayed awake through the long dark, fearful of making the smallest sound as night animals hunted. He prayed silently to his ancestors while his ears strained for sounds of great beasts; the throaty snort of the great bear, the piercing roar of the monster with teeth like long blades.

The dawn found Guff with his head buried within his cloak, ice in his hair. Short puffs of mist escaped from his mouth. When the sun rose above the sharp peaks, Guff felt joy. Despite his aching back, he had faith that he would find his father today. Guff lifted himself from the ditch and walked to the river at the bottom of the ravine. He scooped water in his hands and drank for a long time. He was terribly thirsty and the water was cold and delicious. Guff could feel strength return, the panic of the previous day wash away. He gripped his spear and began to trot across large flat stones that warmed in the morning sun. Guff's father had said that when lost, a river could lead you home. Guff's people could be camped on the banks of this river.

**Scene 4**

Guff followed the curve of the river. His leg throbbed which slowed his pace as he watched for beasts that may be at the water's edge. Apart from a few otters, with eyes like black pebbles, Guff saw nothing. Later that morning, Guff climbed to the top of a cliff that blocked his path and saw much that frightened him. Mountains stretched out to a vast distance, all the way to the big sky. Guff felt like an ant standing upon a newly cured and stretched skin of a muloth. Guff climbed back down into the ravine and once again followed the snake-like river.

He trotted along the river's edge until the mist had left the valley. The sun was directly above Guff when he reached the shore of a large lake. He hoped that the river continued again further down. The lake's surface was calm. Mountain peaks reflected in the lake's icy water and a thin vapour whispered up from the water's surface. The sight of the lake was soothing. Guff's breath was ragged from fatigue and his injured leg throbbed. He was hungry and had not eaten for days. Guff felt he needed to keep moving but he was also very tired. He sat near the lake's surface to rest. His eyes scanned the banks of the lake for movement, but the area was quiet. No bears, no big cats. Near to where Guff rested, were the bones of an elk. It had lain there a long time for the bones were clean and bleached white. Guff lay his head upon a flat stone and closed his eyes.

**Scene 5**

Guff awoke to the sound of tiny splashes, like flat stones skipped across water. He tracked the sound and glimpsed fish darting and breaching the lake's surface to feed on insects. Guff needed a fishing spear, a water spear. He walked slowly to the elk bones; nursing his sore leg. Guff picked out rib bones. These he honed and carved with his blade so that both ends were sharp. Guff cut the bindings of his spear and removed the stone spear tip. He cut new notches into the spear's shaft and attached the newly sculpted rib bones to the wood. Guff then shaped and slotted the bones neatly into the grooves and bound the bones with twine. The spear now featured spikes of sharp bone.

Guff stepped into the bitterly cold water and raised his spear. He balanced and waited, careful not to move. The water nipped his legs, like sharp teeth piercing his skin. He could not stand in this water for long. Guff scanned the surface of the lake for movement. Suddenly, a hint of fin stabbed the surface close to where he stood. Guff launched the spear. Guided by luck, mostly, and some skill it sliced into the flesh of a fish the size of his forearm. Guff hauled the fish into the air and droplets of water sprinkled in his hair. He whooped with excitement and flicked the spear. The fish landed flapping on big stones near the water's edge, its scales glistening in the sun. Guff was relieved to haul his legs from the frigid water. His teeth chattered as he struck the fish's head with a rock. He then removed its scales with his blade. By the time Guff had finished preparing the fish, the sun was low in the sky and the shadows were long. He would travel no further today. Guff did not wish to sleep huddled in the cold this night chewing raw fish. He knew the dangers, but he would cook the fish.

**Scene 6**

Guff gathered leaves, bark and branches from the base of an old tree. He possessed a dark stone that hung safe from his neck, stuck to leather twine by pitch. The stone was sharp and shaped like a leaf. The stone's value was greater than his spear or blade, for the stone made fire. Guff selected a flat rock and placed dried grass on it. He struck the rock with the dark stone. The stone struck at an angle so that sparks landed in the tufts of dry grass.

After some effort, a wisp of smoke appeared. Guff blew on the twist of smoke until a flame stretched and curled. Excited, he layered more grass and thin strips of bark on the tiny flame until it grew. Guff skewered the fish onto a sharpened stick and wrapped it in green leaves from a nearby water plant. He then roasted the fish over the flames. Its aroma made his stomach rumble. Guff removed the fish from the flames, unwrapped the now blackened leaves and picked the flesh from the fish's bones. The flesh was hot and singed Guff's fingers, but it was delicious - charred on the outside, sweet in the middle. Guff finished eating and threw a large branch on the fire. He watched sleepily as sparks and smoke climbed into the twilight air.

## Scene 7

A shadow loomed. Guff could see it out of the corner of his eye. Though Guff could only sense the shadow's dark outline, he felt a spike of pure fear that pierced his heart. The beast prowled slowly, sniffing the air, tracing Guff's scent through the smoke. The creature's head took shape beyond the shroud of smoke. It opened its jaws to reveal terrible long teeth. Guff felt the blood drain from his face. Here was death, a short stone toss from where he sat. If Guff moved too quickly, the beast would see him instantly. Guff never took his eyes off the monster as he slowly sorted his limbs and silently prepared his spear. Guff realized to his dismay that the spear was now only useful for stabbing fish.

Guff's only chance was to reach and climb the old tree. He gave a short prayer to his ancestors and leapt to his feet. Guff then threw the spear at the beast with all his strength. The spear flew true and struck the side of the great cat, just below its shoulder. The force caused the bones bound to the spear to break and scatter like a dandelion seed in a gust of wind. The spear failed to pierce the beast's thick hide. But for a moment, the big cat was off balance. It snarled. Its ears flat against its head. It saw Guff and its yellow eyes narrowed, its muscles tensing. The beast roared and then leapt.

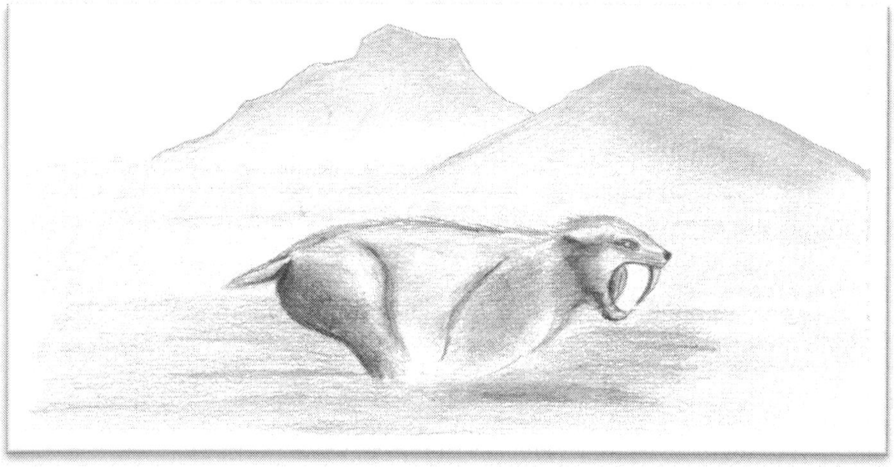

Guff lunged for the tree. In a few strides, he reached the base of the tree. He grasped blindly at the branches above his head. Guff's fingers gripped thick bark and he frantically pulled himself up. An instant later, the tree shuddered as the heavy animal slammed into it. But Guff was just out of reach and the beast could only bellow in frustration. It lurked at the tree's base and stared up at Guff with its fierce eyes.

In the distance, Guff could hear voices, his name called. His name, the most beautiful sound in the world. Startled, the big cat bounded away. Guff looked down through the branches and saw his father and other men from their tribe sprinting to the tree. They had been tracking Guff and had seen the smoke from his fire. A wave of emotion like clear water washed through Guff. He climbed down from the tree and was embraced by his father. They returned that night, weary, to the tribe's camp and Guff's father watched Guff as he slept by a big well-tended fire and was still there when Guff woke the next morning.

# 3

# Reading, Reading Comprehension, and Story Grammar Analysis

# Reading, Reading Comprehension and Story Grammar Analysis

## Objective

1. Introduce reading error analysis.
2. To explain the rationale for Question Comprehension baselines.
3. Introduce the principles of story grammar assessment.

## Analysis of Reading Errors

The reading error analysis screen can provide insight into a student's ability to decode unfamiliar text and can act as a basis for diagnosis for error types and provide a blueprint for effective intervention planning. There are two error categories: accuracy errors and fluency errors. Accuracy reading errors indicate a reader struggles to decode unfamiliar text and so may not be able to adequately access a text's meaning. Fluency related errors may increase when a student encounters a particularly difficult patch of text, which reduces reading rate and also affects comprehension.

### Accuracy Reading Errors

- Words Replaced

  The student substitutes an unfamiliar word he/she cannot decode with a word they do understand.

- Words Added

  The student inserts a word into the reading that is not on the printed page. An added word can change the meaning of a passage.

- Words Deleted

  Words that are on the printed page are omitted, which can change the meaning of a passage.

- Words Incorrect

  The student cannot read a word and abandons all attempts to decode the word.

### Fluency Reading Errors

- **Words Repeated**

  The student repeats a word.

- **Word by Word Reading**

  The student reads word by word, which affects fluency.

- **Pauses While Reading**

  The student pauses while attempting to decode a difficult word.

- **Self Correction**

  The student corrects a previously miscued word.

## Reading Error Analysis Guide

1. The student reads from an unfamiliar text, in this case *Guff's Journey.* The student encounters text that they are unfamiliar with.
2. Record each reading error using the symbols found on the Error Analysis Symbols chart on page 36. The reading session should be recorded with a recording device. Most mobile (cell) phones have a voice recording feature.
3. Find a quiet area. Sit across from the student and ensure that the recording device works properly. The child reads from the selected text.
4. Make certain that you have a photocopy of the selected text so that you can mark errors with the miscue symbols as the student reads from the passage. Prior to the reading assessment, count the number of words in the target passage and record the number of words under Total Words on the record form.
5. Begin the analysis by saying to the student, "Please read this story (or passage) out loud to me in a clear voice. When you come to a word you don't know have a go at working it out, but if you can't work it out then move onto the next word as soon as you can. At the end of the passage, I'm going to ask you a few questions about the passage and then I'll ask you to tell me about the story in as much detail as you can." (Both time and record the session)

6. After the reading is completed, allow the student a few minutes to relax and then begin the comprehension questions. (Refer to the Reading Comprehension Guide on page 39).
7. Once the comprehension questions are complete, the student can provide an oral retell of the story. (Refer to the Story Grammar Guide on page 47)
8. Transcribe the errors from the photocopied passage to the Reading Errors Record Form. Use the example form as a guide if needed. Your mobile (cell) phone should have a calculator in the apps section to calculate the totals.

p **Scene 1**

The dry grass pressed fierce into Guff's legs as he lay in the dirt, but he did not ~~complain~~ company. Guff was on his first hunt with the elders and he needed to be ~~quiet~~ as a ~~field~~ feel mouse. Above the hunters loomed a mighty bull ~~mammoth~~ sc, its tusks curved and lethal. Sweat p beaded Guff's p ~~forehead~~ forrest though the day was cold. Guff's father, Utha, anxious for Guff, met his eyes and smiled. Utha's arm muscles were

## Reading Error Analysis – Example

This section demonstrates a reading error analysis completed with our 10 year old student, Daniel who read from the original story, *Guff's Journey*.

As we can see from the above example, the student made several reading miscues. The reading sample indicates that the student paused when he encountered an unfamiliar word and attempted to decode it. The word complain was miscued as company and the word field was miscued as feel, which changes the meaning of the passage somewhat. The student also deleted the word quiet. The student's overall reading fluency was poor due to the pauses and the word for word reading. The student did self-correct the word mammoth as can be seen with the symbol sc. This short sample demonstrates the usefulness of what is a simple informal test. But even this very short sample gives us an insight into this student's reading difficulty.

## Reading Error Symbols (Accuracy Error Symbols)

| Reading Error | Symbol | Method |
|---|---|---|
| Words Replaced | water<br>~~winter~~ | Draw a line through the replaced word and write the substituted word above. |
| Words Added | snow<br>^ | Draw a small triangle and write the added word above. |
| Words Deleted | ~~silent~~ | Draw a line through the deleted word. |
| Incorrect Words | [range] | Draw a square or circle around the miscued word. |

## Reading Error Symbols (Fluency Errors Symbols)

| Reading Error | Symbol | Method |
|---|---|---|
| Words Repeated | r | Write *r* above any words that are repeated. |
| Word by Word | <u>with</u> <u>silent</u> <u>grace</u> | Draw a line under each word that is read word by word. |
| Self-Correction | sc | Write **sc** above any words that are self-corrected by the reader. |
| Pauses while Reading | p | Use *p* to signal when a student pauses for an extended length of time. |

## Reading Error Record Form

Student: ____________________ Date: ________ Total Words: _________

Reading Time: _______ Reading Rate: ________ (*words per min*). To tally words per minute, count the time it took the student to complete the passage. Then divide the total no. of words in passage by total time (*in seconds*). Reading Rate = no. of words / time x 60.

### Reading Errors *(Accuracy Errors)*

Words Replaced ________ Words Deleted ________

Words Added ________ Words Incorrect ________

Accuracy Errors ________

### Reading Errors *(Fluency Errors)*

Words Repeated ________ Pauses While Reading ________

Word by Word ________

Self-Correction ________

Fluency Errors ________

Add the total number of **accuracy** errors and **fluency** errors.

Combined Errors (ac + fl) _______

Divide **accuracy errors** and **fluency errors** by **combined errors** and multiply by 100 to work out the percentage of errors in a passage.

Like this...

*Accuracy Errors*

No. of **accuracy errors** ____ /_____ **combined errors** = _____ x 100 = _____ % **ac**

*Fluency Errors*

No. of **fluency errors** ____ /_____ **combined errors** = _____ x 100 = _____ % **fl**

## Reading Error Record Form – *Example*

| | | |
|---|---|---|
| Student: Daniel | Date: 12/10/2016 | Total Words: 550 |

Reading Time: 370 secs Reading Rate: 89.20 (*words per min*). To tally words per minute, count the time it took the student to complete the passage. Then divide the total no. of words in passage by total time (*in seconds*). **Reading Rate = no. of words / time x 60.**

### Reading Errors *(Accuracy Errors)*

| | | | |
|---|---|---|---|
| Words Replaced | *5* | Words Deleted | *4* |
| Words Added | *4* | Words Incorrect | *6* |
| Accuracy Errors | *19* | | |

### Reading Errors *(Fluency Errors)*

| | | | |
|---|---|---|---|
| Words Repeated | *2* | Pauses While Reading | *10* |
| Word by Word | *5* | | |
| Self-Corrections | *6* | | |
| Fluency Errors | *23* | | |

Add the total number of **accuracy** errors and **fluency** errors.

Combined Errors (ac + fl) *19+23=42* errors

Divide **accuracy errors** and **fluency errors** by **combined errors** and multiply by 100 to work out the percentage of errors in a passage.

Like this...

*Accuracy Errors*

No. of **accuracy errors** *19 /42* combined errors = 0.45 x 100 = 45 % **ac**

*Fluency Errors*

No. of **fluency errors** *23 /42* combined errors = 0.54 x 100 = 54 % **fl**

## Baselines for Reading Comprehension

Baselines can provide a starting point for language intervention planning. To obtain a baseline level of a student's abilities with oral and written language a clinician must first conduct specific assessments. In this workbook, the two language skills that are assessed are oral and reading comprehension and story grammar.

## Question Comprehension

If a student struggles with decoding, do they also struggle with *comprehension* of text? Targeted inference and story detail questions can help determine this. When establishing a baseline, clinicians and teachers will have a range of potential intervention areas to target if a student struggles with either reading fluency and accuracy or oral comprehension. The question comprehension tasks in this chapter provide a checklist of story detail and inferential questions to examine students' oral and reading comprehension skills.

## Narrative/Story Grammar

Children with language difficulty struggle to produce coherent and detailed oral narratives. In general, children with language difficulty have shorter narratives that lack both detail and complexity. This difficulty also affects the ability of students to infer important information in a story, understand story details, and comprehend narrative sequence. Consequently, students who experience language comprehension difficulties often have poor understanding of a story's setting, a reduced insight into character motivation and exchanges, and their oral narrative retells lack detail and awareness. Analyses of both oral and written narratives are considered macrostructure tasks, in that they assess the overall structure of a student's oral or written retell.

The assessment components will be used to establish a baseline with our fictional 10-year-old school student, Daniel.

**Sample Text**: The sample text will be an excerpt from the story, *Guff's Journey*. To establish a baseline for question comprehension and narrative retell in literature based assessment, there is a sequence of steps that need to be completed.

## Sequence

The student is to read from a selected book targeted at the child's instructional level. The selected book should not be *too easy* to read but also not *too difficult*. The Fleisch Kincaid can be an effective tool in choosing suitable, age appropriate books for an individual student. For the purposes of this book, the story, *Guff's Journey* is the example text.

## Instructions

**Use the following sequence when establishing a question comprehension baseline.**

- Begin the analysis by saying to the student… *"Please read this story (or scene) out loud to me in a clear voice. When you come to a word you don't know have a go at working it out, but if you can't get it then move onto the next word as soon as you can. At the end of the story I'm going to ask you a few questions about the story and then I'll ask you to tell me about the story in as much detail as you can."* (Both time and record the session)

- After the reading is completed, allow the student 5 minutes to relax and then begin the comprehension questions. (Refer to the **Question Comprehension Analysis**).
- Once the comprehension questions are complete, the student is to give an oral retell of the story or the scene or scenes they have read.
- To gain an understanding of students' reading comprehension abilities, it is necessary to spend time generating *factual*, *surface level* inference and *deep level* inference questions from the target text. Read the example provided for some ideas. Questions can be created well before the student begins the assessment. Factual questions can be generated from who, what, and where questions. Inference questions can be a little trickier to generate.

- It is important to note that factual questions centre on what the characters *did* in a story or on the events that happened in a story. Inference questions are generated from events not detailed in the story narrative but hinted at by the author. Correct and accurate answers to inference questions require a deeper understanding of a story's purpose.

- Fact Based Question: A question that has a specific answer and that is clearly stated in the text. (What did the character wear?)

- Surface Level Inference Question: A question which asks about something that is implied or hinted at in the text. (Why was the character frightened?)

- Deep Level Inference Question: A question that does not rely on textual information. The reader must draw on world and word knowledge, and problem solving abilities. (Was the character angry or just playing? Would you be angry in the same situation?)

## Example Questions in Appendix D

A range of example questions that cover the seven scenes in the Guff's Journey story are in appendix D. Each of the seven scenes has three fact based questions, three shallow level inference questions and three deep level inference questions, a total of sixty three questions. The example questions are certainly not exhaustive, but do provide a guide to the type of questions that can be gleaned from the Guff's Journey text. Clinicians and teachers are encouraged to use the example questions as a guide to, in time, develop your own fact based and inference questions.

# Question Comprehension Analysis – *Example*

**Sample Text**: This section demonstrates a question comprehension analysis completed with student Daniel who read the story, *Guff's Journey.*

### Scene 1

The dry grass pressed fierce into Guff's legs as he lay in the dirt, but he did not complain. Guff was on his first hunt with the elders and he needed to be quiet as a field mouse. Above the hunters loomed a mighty bull muloth, its tusks curved and lethal. Sweat beaded Guff's forehead though the day was cold. Guff's father, Utha, anxious for Guff, met his eyes and smiled. Utha's arm muscles were tense and corded as if carved from oak. He lay flat beside other men of the tribe a short spear toss from Guff. Between the tribe's spears and fat calves was the bull.

In the above example text we have part of the first scene of the story. We can generate a number of *factual*, *shallow level inference* and *deep level inference* questions from this short section. The next section features example of questions generated from the *Guff's Journey* text.

There are multiple targets to form questions from this short sample. We have a rather tense scene where Guff lays in the dirt not daring to move or even breathe, the other worldly and exotic location set in prehistoric Europe and the unimaginably tense and terrifying image of a wild mammoth, an animal that would dwarf a modern day elephant, ripping out chunks of grass mere centimetres from the protagonist's head.

Each comprehension analysis form has space provided to write the initial question, the student's verbal response and the score assigned to each response with a handy score guide with *0* for an inaccurate or incomplete response, *1* for partially correct response and a score of *2* assigned to scores that are complete and accurate. Clinicians should use the example pages as a guide to generate questions from other sections or the same section from the *Guff's Journey* story and, eventually, from commercially available storybooks.

# Question Comprehension Analysis – Factual

## *(Example)*

Student: *Michael* Date: *17/10/2016* Year Level: *4*

School: *Mount Bump P.S.* Book Title: *Guff's Journey – SCENE 1*

### Factual Questions

Score each question 0, 1, or 2.

| | |
|---|---|
| Question 1: | What pressed into Guff's legs? |
| Students Response: | *'Dry grass'* |
| Score: | 2 |
| Question 2: | What were the main targets of the hunt? |
| Students Response: | *'The mammoths or muloths'* (Correct answer – *several calves*) |
| Score: | 1 |

Factual Question Score Guide

| | |
|---|---|
| **0** | Inaccurate and incomplete |
| **1** | Partially correct, logical but not complete |

# Question Comprehension Analysis – Surface Level Inference *(Example)*

| | |
|---|---|
| Student: *Michael* | Date: *17/10/2016* Year Level: *4* |
| School: *Mount Bump P.S.* | Book Title: *Guff's Journey – SCENE 1* |

## Surface Inference Questions

Score each question 0, 1, or 2.

| | |
|---|---|
| Question 1: | Why was Guff's forehead slick with sweat? |
| Students Response: | *'He was hot'* (Incorrect answer – Guff is nervous) |
| Score: | 0 |
| Question 2: | Why are the muloth's tusks described as lethal? |
| Students Response: | *'Because they are sharp and long"* |
| Score: | 1 |

| Surface Level Inference Question Score Guide | |
|---|---|
| **0** | Inaccurate and incomplete |
| **1** | Partially correct, logical but not complete |

# Question Comprehension Analysis – Deep Level Inference *(Example)*

| | | |
|---|---|---|
| Student: *Michael* | Date: *17/10/2016* | Year Level: *4* |
| School: *Mount Bump P.S.* | Book Title: *Guff's Journey – SCENE 1* | |

## Deep Level Inference Questions

Score each question 0, 1, or 2.

Question 1: Why was it important for hunters to be very quiet when hunting?

Students Response: *'Too much noise might scare away the animals'*

Score: 2

Question 2: For what reason would Neanderthals be hunting mammoths (muloths), particularly when they are so dangerous?

Students Response: *'Because they are hungry'* (Partially true – hunger, clothing, expert hunters)

Score: 1

| Deep Level Inference Question Score Guide | |
|---|---|
| 0 | Inaccurate and incomplete |
| 1 | Partially correct, logical but not complete |

# Analysis of Comprehension Responses

## Factual Based Questions

As we can see with responses of fictional student, Daniel, he did quite well with factual questions related to simple, literal information. For the three factual questions the student scored nearly full marks. His only error was that he believed the mammoths' were the target of the hunt. The more accurate response would be that the calves were the target of the hunt.

## Surface Level Inference Questions

The student struggled with questions that required him to interpret information that was present in the text. His understanding of *surface level inference* questions was average in that he understood the premise of the question but was unable to supply detailed information. He scored *3 points* out of a possible *6*.

## Deep Level Inference Questions

The student struggled to answer the inference questions. The student's response to the question, *'How old do you think Guff might be?'* is revealing in that the student believes Guff to be much younger than he actually is. Of course, with deep level inference questions there may be several correct answers to a question. In this instance, the student may not have the world knowledge or awareness to know that a very young child would *most likely* not be on a hunt with grown men particularly as they hunt large and dangerous mammoths.

On the basis of this brief analysis of question comprehension skills, we can conclude that the student's comprehension of the story's more complex themes is quite poor. The student is able to recognize and attend to the surface details of the text but doesn't have the language skills or inferential comprehension to unlock the story's deeper themes.

# Oral Retell - Story Grammar Analysis

Children with language comprehension difficulty may have difficulty understanding and explaining story action and events, character motives and sequence of events. The accurate retelling of a recently read story also indicates that students with oral language comprehension difficulty may struggle to understand cause/affect structures within stories. The ability to comprehend and accurately identify the structure of complex texts is difficult for students who struggle to understand story grammar structure. Story grammar skills often need to be explicitly taught.

## Sequence

After the student has read the nominated story or scene or has had the story read to them, allow the student to have a short break.

**Instructions:** Use the following sequence when establishing a story grammar baseline.

1. Ensure that you record the child's story retell. Most mobile (cell) phones have apps that allow you to record voices, or you can use a specially designed dictaphone to record students' voices.

**Instructions:** 'Let's look at this story together. It's a story set in prehistoric times about a boy named Guff. You need to listen carefully while I tell the story. When I've finished it will then be your turn to tell the story. Tell me everything you can about the story and make it the best you can.'

2. Transcribe the student's oral retell and score the student's response on the **Oral Retell Macrostructure Analysis** chart.

# Oral Retell Story Grammar Analysis - *Example*

**Sample Text:** This section demonstrates an oral retell of a 10 year old student who narrates the story, *Guff's Journey* after having read the story with the clinician during a shared reading activity five minutes previously.

**Student:** 'There was a boy hunting with his dad. They were hunting mammoths. The boy got lost because a mammoth tried to hurt him. His dad got lost too. The boy fell down a hill and wakes up in a ditch. And he keeps waking up. He's scared cause there's no one there and he's all alone. He wants to go home. He finds a river and then finds a lake. He makes a fire and catches a fish to eat. A big cat sees him and chases him up a tree. He then gets rescued.'

The student's oral retell of *Guff's Journey* is recorded and later transcribed on to the *Story Retell Transcription* form. As we can see from the above example, the student has provided a retell that has some elements of story grammar but the retell is brief and lacks detail.

The grammar is poor and the student's vocabulary is below average for his age and there is very little complex language. The student's oral retell is analysed and his results entered onto the *Oral Retell Macrostructure Analysis* form.

# Oral Retell *Guff's Journey* - Transcription

Student: Daniel DOB: 10/ 09/ 2005 Examiner: David Newman

School: Mount Bump Primary School Date: 17/10/2016

Record the student's oral retell of the story. Most modern cell or mobile phones have a voice recording app as standard, which can record a student's oral retell. Transcribe the student's retell onto the space provided.

Instructions: 'Let's look at this story together. It's a story set in prehistoric times about a boy named Guff. You need to listen carefully while I tell the story. When I've finished it will then be your turn to tell the story. Tell me everything you can about the story and make it the best you can.'

**Student's response**

'There was a boy hunting with his dad. They were hunting mammoths. The boy got lost because a mammoth tried to hurt him. His dad got lost too.

The boy fell down a hill and wakes up in a ditch. And he keeps waking up. He's scared cause there's no one there and he's all alone. He wants to go home.

He finds a river and then finds a lake. He makes a fire and catches a fish to eat. A big cat sees him and chases him up a tree. He then gets rescued.'

# Oral Retell – Macrostructure Analysis Example

| Story Element | Present | Absent |
|---|---|---|
| Beginning<br>(One day, Once upon a time…) | | √ |
| Character Introduction<br>Guff and his father Utha | √ | |
| Initiating Event<br>(Guff is on his first hunt…) | | √ |
| Plan: Cognitive verb used…<br>(Guff knew he needed to be quiet….) | | √ |
| 1. Attempt to solve the problem<br>(Guff ran for his life to escape the mammoth) | | √ |
| Obstacle<br>(Guff fall down a hill and lands in a ditch…) | √ | |
| 2. Attempt to solve the problem<br>(Guff follows a river to find his tribe and home…) | | √ |
| Consequence<br>(Guff makes a fire to cook a fish and attracts a saber-toothed cat) | | √ |
| Reaction/Resolution<br>(Guff races to a tree and climbs up to escape the saber-toothed cat) | | √ |
| Closing Event<br>(The fire has been seen by Guff's tribe who rescue Guff from the big cat.) | | √ |

Indicate the level of prompts needed for the student to complete the oral retell. Please tick the appropriate box that best represented the use of prompts.

- ☐ None: The student completed the oral retell effectively without prompts.
- ☐ General prompts: The student needed some prompts, *'you're doing well…'*
- ☐ Specific prompts: *'Tell me how the story begins …how did he feel?*

# Oral Retell – Macrostructure Analysis Form

| Story Element | Present | Absent |
|---|---|---|
| **Beginning**<br>(One day, Once upon a time…) | | |
| **Character Introduction**<br>Guff and his father Utha | | |
| **Initiating Event**<br>(Guff is on his first hunt…) | | |
| **Plan: Cognitive verb used…**<br>(Guff knew he needed to be quiet….) | | |
| **1. Attempt to solve the problem**<br>(Guff ran for his life to escape the mammoth) | | |
| **Obstacle**<br>(Guff fall down a hill and lands in a ditch…) | | |
| **2. Attempt to solve the problem**<br>(Guff follows a river to find his tribe and home…) | | |
| **Consequence**<br>(Guff makes a fire to cook a fish and attracts a saber tooth cat) | | |
| **Reaction/Resolution**<br>(Guff races to a tree and climbs up to escape the saber-tooth cat) | | |
| **Closing Event**<br>(The fire has been seen by Guff's tribe who rescue Guff from the big cat.) | | |

Indicate the level of prompts needed for the student to complete the oral retell. Please tick the appropriate box that best represented the use of prompts.

- ☐ **None**: The student completed the oral retell effectively without prompts.
- ☐ **General prompts**: The student needed some prompts, *'you're doing well…'*
- ☐ **Specific prompts**: *'Tell me how the story begins …how did he feel?*

# 4

# Building Pre-Story Background Information

# Pre-Story Background Information

Instructions: Read the information about Neanderthal man and the prehistoric world with your students. The goal here is to provide background information about the elements that make up the prehistoric world that is featured in *Guff's Journey*.

Prehistoric World: *Guff's Journey* is set in the prehistoric world about 100,000 years ago, during the late Pleistocene period when glaciers still covered much of Europe. The prehistoric world of this epoch was a harsh place. Humanoid tribes such as Neanderthal and early modern man competed for scarce resources in a formidable and hostile environment. Europe at that time was still in the grip of an ice age though the world was slowly thawing. Neanderthal man had to battle the tough climate, hunt herds of megafauna such as mammoths and giant elk to survive and avoid fearsome predators like the saber-toothed cat and cave bear.

Neanderthal man: Neanderthals were a species of prehistoric human that lived in Europe and parts of Northern Africa about 100,000 years ago. Neanderthals had similar features to modern humans but differed in that they had much more robust bodies, and bigger brains. Researchers of prehistoric man believe that Neanderthals could speak and used complex forms of verbal and sign language. Neanderthals were a nomadic people, in that they moved from place to place to hunt herds of animals and to survive. They were excellent hunters and could make fire to keep warm. Neanderthal man used tools such as axes and spears, which they carved from stone and bone and were very sharp. The Neanderthal people mostly dressed in clothes that they created and fashioned from animal hide.

**Wooly Mammoth:** The wooly mammoth was a prehistoric type of elephant that lived in the late Pleistocene period. The mammoth had a different appearance to modern elephants in that the mammoth was much larger than a modern elephant and was covered in long hair. The mammoth had much smaller ears than a modern elephant. The ears were shorter and smaller to prevent frostbite and reduce heat loss in the harsh climate. Mammoths had massive curved tusks that were much longer than modern elephant tusks. Several frozen carcasses of fully preserved mammoths have been uncovered in Siberia and Alaska. These finds have allowed scientists to study mammoth physiology and eating habits in great detail. Mammoths lived during the same period of history as Neanderthal man who used mammoth hide for making clothing and mammoth bones and tusks to construct shelter and tools. Within the context of the *Guff's Journey* story, the Neanderthal people refer to the mammoth as a *muloth*.

**Saber-Toothed Cat:** The saber-toothed cat was a ferocious predator that lived in the late Pleistocene period. Saber-toothed cats had enormous tearing teeth on their upper jaw that gave them a menacing appearance. The cat's massive front teeth could grow to as long as 30 centimeters. The teeth protruded from the creature's mouth even when the mouth was closed. Saber-toothed cats were stocky in build, almost bear like. They were unlike modern big cats such as cats and lions, because they were not sleek and slender but broad and thickset. The saber-toothed cat became extinct about 10,000 years ago.

# Background Information Questions

Read the following questions to your students and discuss the answers. You can also link extra information about Neanderthal man and his environment by accessing other texts, or find information online such as Wikipedia.

**Question 1:** Where in the world did Neanderthal man live?

______________________________________________

**Question 2:** How did Neanderthal man differ from modern humans?

______________________________________________

**Question 3:** Did Neanderthal man stay in one place, or did they move often? How do you know this?

______________________________________________

**Question 4:** What types of tools did Neanderthal man use?

______________________________________________

**Question 5:** What did Neanderthal man use for clothes?

______________________________________________

**Question 6:** What were Neanderthals excellent at doing?

______________________________________________

**Question 7:** What modern animal is a mammoth similar to?

______________________________________________

**Question 8:** With what were mammoths covered?

______________________________________________

**Question 9:** What are saber-toothed cats famous for having on their upper jaws?

______________________________________________

**Question 10:** Were saber-toothed cats broad and thickset or sleek and slender?

______________________________________________

# Inference Questions

**Question 1:** Why were mammoths covered in long hair?

---

**Question 2:** Would there have been towns and cities 100,000 years ago? Why/why not?

---

**Question 3:** Did Neanderthals cook their food?

---

**Question 4:** Could Neanderthals read and write?

---

**Question 5:** Do you think the Neanderthals feared the saber-toothed cat? Why/why not?

---

**Question 6:** For what purpose did Neanderthals use axes and spears?

---

**Question 7:** Were Neanderthals able to communicate with each other? How did they communicate?

---

**Question 8:** Could a Neanderthal survive in the wilderness much better than a modern human could? Why/why not?

---

**Question 9:** Did Neanderthal man prefer to settle and live in one place? Why/why not? What tells us this?

---

# Exploring Themes – Pre-Story Background Map

The pre-story background map is an excellent means of exploring many of the background themes of a story. This section details how to use the map to target and discuss some of the themes and setting of *Guff's Journey* to assist students' understanding of the prehistoric world. As we can see from our example, the clinician has chosen three main themes to be discussed with the student prior to the reading of the text. The three main themes are *Neanderthal man*, *mighty animals* and *harsh climate*.

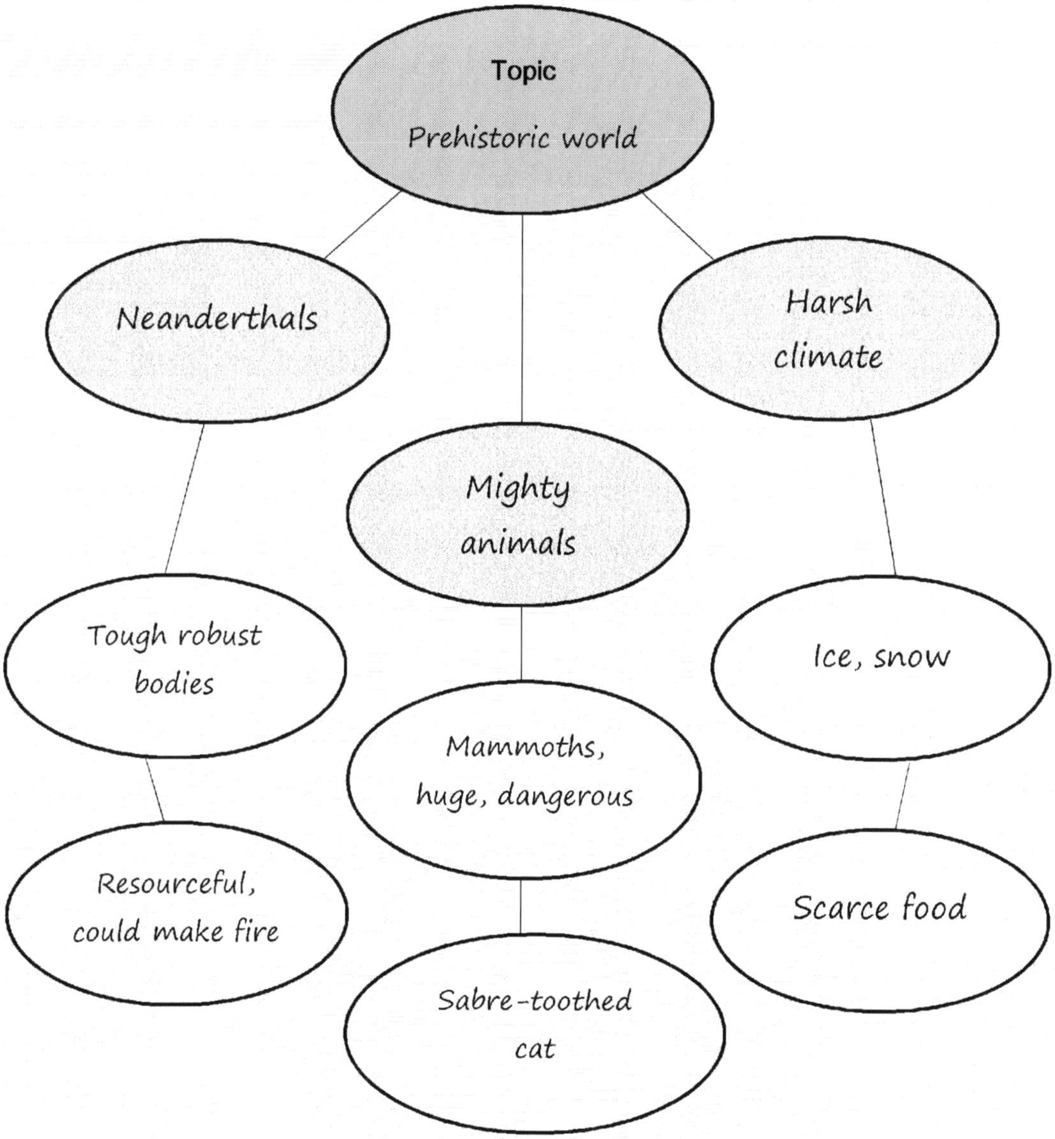

# Pre-story Background Map Discussion - *Example*

The clinician begins the learning session by writing the three target themes for the pre-story discussion: *Neanderthal man, mighty animals* and *harsh climate*. The clinician writes the three themes into the shaded boxes on the pre-story map.

**Clinician**: 'Guff's Journey is an exciting story set in the prehistoric world about 100,000 years ago. Do you know what prehistoric refers to Daniel?'

**Daniel**: 'Not sure.'

**Clinician**: 'Well, history refers to everything that has happened in our past. In the history of people I mean. We're pretty sure what happened up to 5000 years ago but history becomes very difficult to learn about before that time because early humans did not read nor write so left no written history of their time. Prehistory or prehistoric means that we have only clues about the people and animals of about 100,000 years ago, mainly from bones and fossils.'

The clinician refers to the pre-story map and points to the three target themes that were written previously.

**Clinician**: 'Guff's Journey is a story about Neanderthal man. We learnt a little about what Neanderthals were previously. But to summarize, Neanderthal man was a species of early human, similar to modern man but with some differences. Can you remember what some of the differences were Daniel?'

**Daniel**: 'Um, they were big and strong and were good at hunting stuff.'

**Clinician**: 'That's right. Neanderthal man were expert hunters. They hunted mammoths and other large animals. They must have been tough to survive in those times and we know they were stronger than modern man because their bones tell us they were bigger and tougher.'

The clinician writes the words *tough, robust bodies* into the circular box directly beneath the box for *Neanderthal man.*

**Clinician**: 'We also know that Neanderthal man could make fire and they must have been resourceful to survive in the ice age, because it was very cold.'

The clinician writes the words *resourceful* and *could make fire* into the box directly beneath the previous two boxes. This concludes the pre-story for Neanderthal man. The clinician then begins work on the next theme, *mighty animals.*

**Clinician**: '*Mighty animals* refers to the megafauna of that time. Many of the large animals from 100,000 years ago are now extinct. Two of the extinct animals from that time feature in Guff's Journey. The animals are the wooly mammoth and the saber-toothed cat. What do we know about the mammoth?'

**Daniel**: 'It's like a big hairy elephant.'

**Clinician**: 'That's right. They were like modern elephants in some ways. Mammoths were huge animals with long curved tusks and were hairy. The long hair was to protect and insulate them from the extreme cold of the ice age. The other animal that turns up in the story is the saber-toothed cat. What did we learn previously about the saber-toothed cat?'

**Daniel**: 'It has really long teeth and it's scary.'

**Clinician**: 'Yes, saber-toothed cats were fierce predators that hunted large animals and we can assume that Neanderthal man were frightened of the big cats and learnt to keep well away from them.'

The clinician next points to the final theme to be explored with the pre-story background map: the harsh environment.

**Clinician**: 'Though it is not stated directly in the story, the setting for Guff's Journey is during the latter stages of an ice age in prehistoric Europe. The weather was often icy which is why we see Guff rugged up in animal furs. This must have been a tough environment to live in and we can imagine it would have taken a lot of skill and resilience to survive in such a difficult place, because food may have been scarce.'

The clinician fills in the final pre-story boxes. The clinician next turns the pages of Guff's Journey and discusses all of the pictures with Daniel. The clinician also scaffolds questions to assist Daniel to identify the main plot points in the story.

# 5

# Recall of Story Details

# Recall of Story Details

The questions in this section prompt students to reflect on the text. There are three types of questions, Story Details, Moments in Time and Inferences from the Story. The text has been divided into seven scenes for ease of access to particular sequences in the story.

**Recall of Story Details:** The questions relate to specific actions or descriptions in the story. The questions are literal and require a surface level understanding of the text to comprehend. If students have difficulty at any point with these questions, it is recommended that the student reread the scene.

**Moments in Time:** As the title suggests, moments in time refers to an understanding of time and the sequence of events in the story. Students' understanding of story sequence is a critical factor in comprehending complex storylines. The questions prompt students to think of what happened first and next in a particular scene. The questions also probe whether an action happened before or after a related sequence of actions. If students struggle with this section, scaffold the questions by reading the scene again and commenting on the sequence.

**Inferences from the Story:** Inference questions stimulate students' higher order thinking skills and impel students to go beyond surface level skimming of text to explore an author's use of language. Inference questions prompt students to uncover hidden information that is hinted at in the text, but not stated explicitly.

**Important note:** Many of the questions are complex in nature, particularly the moments in time questions that require students to consider sequence of events in order, which can be a difficult task. With this in mind, repeat the questions as often as is needed, or reread the target scene several times so that students have the opportunity to accurately place the order of key scenes. Also, have a copy of the scene so that the student can scan the text for the correct information

# Story Details

## Scene 1

1. How close was Guff to his father as they lay in the dirt?

    ______________________________

2. What pressed into Guff's leggings as he lay in the dirt?

    ______________________________

3. What did the mammoths graze upon?

    ______________________________

4. What did the mammoth's breath do to Guff's hair?

    ______________________________

5. What did the bull mammoth suddenly do?

    ______________________________

6. What were the bull mammoth's tusks described as being?

    ______________________________

7. Who was Utha lying next to?

    ______________________________

# Moments in Time

## Scene 1

1. Which happened first, Guff's heart flipped like a fish or Utha smiled?

   ______________________________________________

2. Did Guff describe his forehead as being slick with sweat before or after he needed to be as a quiet as a field mouse?

   ______________________________________________

3. Did the mammoth approach the grass near Guff before or after Utha smiled to calm Guff?

   ______________________________________________

4. Which happened first, Guff's heart thumped fierce or the stink of the mammoth's shaggy mane filled Guff's senses?

   ______________________________________________

5. Did the mammoth tear out chunks of grass before or after its breath rippled Guff's hair?

   ______________________________________________

# Making Inferences from the Story

## Scene 1

1. Why did Guff's father Utha smile at Guff as they lay in the grass?

________________________________________________

2. Why did Guff need to be as quiet as a field mouse?

________________________________________________

3. How do we know that the mammoth was very close to Guff as it tore chunks of grass?

________________________________________________

4. Why did Guff's heart thump fierce when the mammoth walked close to where he lay?

________________________________________________

5. Guff describes the day as being cool. Why do you think his forehead was slick with sweat?

________________________________________________

# Story Details

## Scene 2

1. What was Utha doing above all the confusion?

___

2. What did Guff have no memory of?

___

3. What happened to Guff after he was hit in the side?

___

4. What did Guff describe as happening to him after he struck the hard dirt?

___

5. What did Guff fail to see because he was panicking?

___

6. What happened to Guff's legs as he ran?

___

7. Where was Guff at the end of scene 2?

___

# Moments in Time

## Scene 2

1. What happened first, the spears soared and buzzed or a force rigid and powerful hit Guff in the side?

_______________________________________________

2. Which happened first, Guff felt the air ripped from his chest or Guff could hear Utha above the confusion trying to find him?

_______________________________________________

3. When did Guff realize he had lost his father and uncle, *before* or *after* he fell down the steep hill?

_______________________________________________

4. Which happened first, Guff watched the last wisps of gold and warmth cling to the peaks or he poked his head above the ditch?

_______________________________________________

5. Which happened first, Guff's head cleared or he lay in a deep feint?

_______________________________________________

# Making Inferences from the Story

## Scene 2

1. What do you think hit Guff in the side that caused him to soar through the air?

_______________________________________________

2. Why do you think Guff was unable to form words when he tried to call to his father?

_______________________________________________

3. Why do you think Guff failed to see that the ground vanished from under him?

_______________________________________________

4. Why do you think Utha would be pleased with Guff for not losing his blade?

_______________________________________________

5. Why was Guff afraid?

_______________________________________________

# Story Details

## Scene 3

1. What did Guff first have to do before he could search for his tribe at dawn?

   ______________________________

2. What was Guff fearful of making as he lay cold and alone in the ditch?

   ______________________________

3. Who did Guff pray to for help?

   ______________________________

4. What did Guff strain his ears *for* during the long dark?

   ______________________________

5. Where did Guff have his head when dawn arrived?

   ______________________________

6. What did the water taste like from the river?

   ______________________________

7. What had Guff's father told him about rivers if he were ever lost?

   ______________________________

# Moments in Time

## Scene 3

1. Did Guff drink water from the river before or after his recollection of his father's words about make no sound?

   ______________________________________________

2. Which did Guff do first, wrap himself in his furs or listen for sounds of dangerous beasts?

   ______________________________________________

3. Which happened first, short gusts of mist escaped from Guff's mouth or he scooped water into his hands to drink?

   ______________________________________________

4. Did Guff drink the water before or after he left the ditch, where he had been sheltering?

   ______________________________________________

5. Which happened first, Guff gripped his spear or walked to the river at the bottom of the ravine?

   ______________________________________________

# Making Inferences from the Story

## Scene 3

1. How might Guff have felt to be alone in a strange place?

________________________________________

2. Why do you think Guff felt joy when the sun rose above the peaks?

________________________________________

3. Why did Guff pray to his ancestors that night?

________________________________________

4. What tells us that the night had been very cold?

________________________________________

5. What do you think the monster with teeth like long blades as Guff describes it could be?

________________________________________

6. Why was it so important that Guff listened for sounds of wild and dangerous animals that night?

________________________________________

# Story Details

## Scene 4

1. What did Guff watch for as he followed the curve of the river?

______________________________________________

2. What did Guff see when he walked to the top of the cliff?

______________________________________________

3. Where was Guff when the sun was directly above him?

______________________________________________

4. What did Guff describe the lake's surface as being like?

______________________________________________

5. What did Guff climb down into?

______________________________________________

6. What did Guff see near to where he rested?

______________________________________________

7. What did Guff do when he reached the shores of the lake?

______________________________________________

# Moments in Time

## Scene 4

1. Did Guff watch for animals at the water's edge *before* or *after* he climbed to the top of the cliff?

_______________________________________________

2. Which happened first, Guff's leg throbbed or he lay his head upon a flat rock to rest?

_______________________________________________

3. Which did Guff do first, climb the cliff or see the lake?

_______________________________________________

4. When did Guff see the elk bones, *before* or *after* he found the lake?

_______________________________________________

5. When did Guff see the mountains reflected in the lake's icy water, *before* or *after* he saw the elk bones?

_______________________________________________

# Making Inferences from the Story

## Scene 4

1. Why did Guff feel like an ant when he climbed to the top of the cliff?

   ______________________________

2. Was Guff concerned when the river ended and emptied into the lake?

   ______________________________

3. When the sun was directly above Guff at what time of the day was it likely to have been?

   ______________________________

4. Why do you think Guff described the lake as being soothing?

   ______________________________

5. Why was Guff feeling uneasy when he first sat down to rest?

   ______________________________

# Story Details

## Scene 5

1. What caused Guff to wake up?

   ______________________________

2. What was making the little splashes in the lake?

   ______________________________

3. What did Guff have to make?

   ______________________________

4. What did Guff need to create to catch the fish?

   ______________________________

5. What did Guff do to the fish once he had speared it?

   ______________________________

6. What did Guff decide to do after he had caught the fish?

   ______________________________

7. Where was the sun in the sky by the time Guff cleaned the fish?

   ______________________________

# Moments in Time

## Scene 5

1. When did Guff make the water spear, *before* or *after* the splashing woke him up?

   ______________________________________________

2. What did Guff do first, bind the sharpened elk bones to the spear shaft or step into the water?

   ______________________________________________

3. Which happened first, Guff hauled the fish onto the stones near the water's edge or Guff decided to make a fire?

   ______________________________________________

4. Which did Guff do first, clean the fish or make the water spear?

   ______________________________________________

5. When did Guff's stomach grumble and groan, before he heard the fish splashing or after?

   ______________________________________________

# Making Inferences from the Story

## Scene 5

1. Why did Guff's stomach grumble?

2. Why did Guff not wish to stay in the water for too long?

3. Why did Guff not wish to travel any more that day?

4. Was it late in the day by the time Guff had cleaned and scaled the fish? How do you know this?

5. Why was Guff confident he could make a water spear?

# Story Details

## Scene 6

1. What did Guff gather at the base of the old tree?

___

2. What did Guff describe as being shaped like a leaf?

___

3. What landed in the tufts of dried glass?

___

4. What appeared after much effort by Guff?

___

5. What did Guff layer on the flame to make it grow?

___

6. What did the fish taste like?

___

7. After eating the fish, what did Guff throw on the fire?

___

# Moments in Time

## Scene 6

1. When did Guff gather bark and leaves from the base of the old tree, *before* or *after* he struck the rock with the flat stone?

2. What did Guff do first, layer thin strips of bark and twigs onto the flame or skewer the fish onto a sharpened stick?

2. What did Guff do first, layer thin strips of bark and twigs onto the flame or skewer the fish onto a sharpened stick?

3. What did Guff do first, throw a large branch onto the fire or quickly blow on the small wisp of smoke?

4. Which did Guff do first, unwrap the blackened leaves or roast the fish over the flames?

5. When did Guff strike the flat rock with his dark stone, *before* or *after* he roasted the fish over the flames?

# Making Inferences from the Story

## Scene 6

1. What could happen if sparks land in tufts of dried grass?

______________________________________________

2. Why did Guff quickly blow on the wisp of smoke?

______________________________________________

3. What may have happened to the fire if Guff had thrown large branches on the tiny wisp of flame, instead of dried grass and thin strips of bark?

______________________________________________

4. Why do you think Guff wrapped the fish in large green leaves?

______________________________________________

5. It states in the text that Guff was excited. Why do you think Guff was excited to make the fire?

______________________________________________

# Story Details

## Scene 7

1. What loomed from behind the smoke at the edge of the lake?

_______________________________________________

2. What happened to Guff's face when he recognized the beast?

_______________________________________________

3. What could Guff see when the creature opened its jaws?

_______________________________________________

4. What was the cat attempting to do near the fire?

_______________________________________________

5. What did Guff realize to his dismay?

_______________________________________________

6. What did Guff describe as being his only chance of survival against the big cat?

_______________________________________________

7. What did the big cat do when it could not reach Guff in the tree?

_______________________________________________

# Moments in Time

## Scene 7

1. When did Guff desperately climb the tree, *before* or *after* he threw the spear with all his strength?

_______________________________________________

2. What did the big cat do first, sniff the air or launch itself at Guff?

_______________________________________________

3. Which happened first, all the blood drained from Guff's face or the creature sniffed the air?

_______________________________________________

4. Which did Guff do first, sort his limbs and prepare his spear or throw the spear with all his strength?

_______________________________________________

5. When did Guff pray to his ancestors, *before* or *after* he threw the spear at the big cat?

_______________________________________________

# Making Inferences from the Story

## Scene 7

1. What does *'Guff felt the blood drain from his face'* mean?

   ________________________________________________

2. Why did Guff not simply run for his life?

   ________________________________________________

3. What may have happened to Guff if he did not think his way calmly through the situation and *not* distract the big cat?

   ________________________________________________

4. Why do you think Guff described the distant voices calling his name as the most beautiful sound in the world?

   ________________________________________________

5. Why did Guff's father watch over Guff as he slept that night?

   ________________________________________________

# 6

# Syntax and Grammar

# Task A: *Present - Regular Past Tense Verbs*

Change the verbs from **present tense** to **past tense** below by adding – *ed* to the target verb/s. You can use the text as reference if needed. Encourage students to produce past tense verb exercises without first consulting the text. Example: *'Guff's heart* ***flips*** *like a fish when the bull mammoth suddenly* ***stomps*** *close to where he* ***lies****,'* becomes...Guff's heart **flipped** like a fish when the bull mammoth suddenly **stomped** close to where he **lay**.' The first exercise has been completed for you.

1. The dry grass **pressed** fierce into Guff's legs.

   pressed

2. The mammoths **graze** on the long sweet grass, unaware of the hunters.

   ______________________________

3. Above the hunters **looms** a mighty mammoth

   ______________________________

4. The giant was close enough that the snort of its breath **ripples** Guff's hair.

   ______________________________

5. The stink of its shaggy mane **fills** Guff's senses.

   ______________________________

6. Sweat **beads** Guff's forehead.

   ______________________________

7. Guff's heart **thumps** fierce.

________________________________________________________

8. Spears **soar** and **buzz** through the air like insects.

________________________________________________________

9. Guff **tries** to call him but his mouth **fails** to form the words.

________________________________________________________

10. Guff **senses** rather than **sees** something enormous shadow him.

________________________________________________________

11. The fogginess in Guff's head **clears**.

________________________________________________________

12. Guff **shivers**, **huddling** in his furs.

________________________________________________________

13. Guff slowly **sort s** his limbs and silently **prepares** his spear.

________________________________________________________

14. The monster **snarls** and **bounds** away.

________________________________________________________

# Task B: *Present - Irregular Past Tense Verbs*

Change the verbs from **present tense** verbs to **irregular past tense** verbs. Again, you can use the text as reference if needed. Example: *'Guff's forehead runs slick with sweat'* becomes... *'Guff's forehead ran slick with sweat.'* The first exercise has been completed for you.

1. The dry grass pressed fierce into Guff's legs as he **lay** in the dirt.

   The dry grass pressed fierce into Guff's legs as he **lies** in the dirt.

2. Guff **runs** blindly...

   ______________________________

3. Guff **gets** to his feet.

   ______________________________

4. Guff could **hear** shouts from members of the tribe...

   ______________________________

5. Guff **binds** the bones with twine.

   ______________________________

6. Guff **stands** very still.

   ______________________________

7. Guff lifted the fish out of the water and **flings** it onto the riverbank.

---

8. Guff **sees** nothing.

---

9. Guff **throws** some dried leaves on the flame and gently **blows** on it.

---

10. The leaves **catch** fire.

---

11. Guff could **feel** the rhythmic crunch of its legs impact the ground just behind him.

---

12. The half-light before dark **creeps** with long fingers across the land.

---

13. Mountains **rise** sharp and pitiless on all sides.

---

# Task C: *Choose the Correct Word*

Task C: *Correct Word*

Choose the correct word for each sentence. The first one has been completed as a guide.

1. Guff hunted the **bear** with his spear. — *bear* *bare*

2. Asa stuck ________ on her fishing line. — *bait* *bate*

3. Guff ran until his ________ ached. — *mussels* *muscles*

4. Guff cooked the ________ over the fire. — *meet* *meat*

5. Utha couldn't see Guff in the ________. — *mist* *missed*

6. Guff slept through the ________. — *night* *knight*

7. Guff's leg was in ________ after his foot slipped down a hole. — *pain* *pane*

8. Guff gave a ________ of fish to Asa. — peace piece

9. Asa ________ the water into a jug. *poored* *poured*

10. The saber-toothed cat hunted its _______. *pray* *prey*

11. The dark clouds opened and it began to _____. *rain* *rein*

12. Asa made a trap to catch the __________. *hair* *hare*

13. Guff waded through the long __________. *reeds* *reads*

14. Utha __________ the boat down the stream. *road* *rowed*

15. Asa ____________ the seeds in the ground. *sewed* *sowed*

16. Guff felt cold. The ____________ was starting to turn. *weather* *whether*

17. Guff walked across the __________ ground. *rough* *ruff*

18. Guff had ____________ into a strong young man. grown groan

| | | | |
|---|---|---|---|
| 19. | Asa _________the net out of the water. | *halled* | *hauled* |
| 20. | Guff retreated as the _________ cat advanced. | *great* | *grate* |
| 21. | Utha's________beat quickly as he hunted the mammoth. | *hart* | *heart* |
| 22. | Asa picked a wild _________ from the field. | *flour* | *flower* |
| 23. | Guff was given his _________ spear by his proud father. | *knew* | *new* |
| 24. | Guff wanted to _________ as the cat approached. | *flea* | *flee* |
| 25. | Guff ducked as the eagle _________ overhead. | *flu* | *flew* |
| 26. | Guff noticed that the _________ was about to change. | *weather* | *whether* |
| 27. | Asa_______the rug until it was clean. | *beat* | *beet* |
| 28. | Guff's tribe carefully approached the ___________ of mammoths. | heard | herd |

# Task D: *Syntax Exercises*

Create compound sentences from simple sentences using coordinating conjunctions.

The task for this exercise is to combine short simple sentences into compound sentences. Compound sentences are connected together by coordinating conjunctions such as *but*, *and*, *so*, etc. Encourage students to use *pronouns* for some sentences. For instance, *"Guff had greasy fingers so Guff cleaned his hands,"* looks better written as, *"Guff had greasy fingers so he cleaned his hands."*

1. and The water was cold. The air was crisp.

   Example: *The water was cold **and** the air was crisp.*

2. but Guff walked quickly. He didn't get far.

   ________________________________________

3. so The fish ate the bait. Asa caught the fish.

   ________________________________________

4. or Guff could take his axe. Guff could take his spear.

   ________________________________________

5. yet Asa fished all day. Asa didn't catch a fish.

   ________________________________________

| | | | |
|---|---|---|---|
| 6. | but | Utha chased the deer. | Utha couldn't get close. |

______________________________

| | | | |
|---|---|---|---|
| 7. | and | The forest was dark. | The ground was wet. |

______________________________

| | | | |
|---|---|---|---|
| 8. | or | Asa could go fishing. | Asa could go hunting. |

______________________________

| | | | |
|---|---|---|---|
| 9. | but | The cliff was steep. | Guff felt confident. |

______________________________

| | | | |
|---|---|---|---|
| 10. | and | Guff's boots were torn. | Guff's spear was broken. |

______________________________

| | | | |
|---|---|---|---|
| 11. | so | Utha was hungry. | Utha ate some meat. |

______________________________

| | | | |
|---|---|---|---|
| 12. | but | The day was cloudy. | The day was hot. |

______________________________

| | | | |
|---|---|---|---|
| 13. | and | Asa carried her fishing rod. | Asa carried her basket. |
| 14. | yet | Guff climbed the tree. | Guff could not reach the nest. |
| 15. | so | Asa cleaned the fish. | Asa could eat the fish. |
| 16. | and | Guff threw his spear. | Guff took aim. |
| 17. | but | Guff couldn't get warm. | Guff made a fire. |
| 18. | so | Guff climbed a tree | Guff stole bird eggs. |
| 19. | and | Asa filled her jug with water. | Asa walked to the river. |

# Task E: *Syntax Exercises*

Task E: *Contracting Compound Sentences*

The task for this exercise is to break down compound sentences into short simple sentences. The goal is for students to become familiar with the construction of compound sentences and note how they differ from simple sentences.

1. Guff caught the fish and Asa cleaned it.

   Example: *Guff caught the fish.*

   *Asa cleaned the fish.*

2. Asa helped her mother to cook and her father to make a fire.

   ________________________________________

   ________________________________________

3. Guff climbed the mountain and looked out over the ocean.

   ________________________________________

   ________________________________________

4. The eagle swooped down but narrowly missed Guff's head.

   ________________________________________

   ________________________________________

5. Guff wanted to walk but Asa wanted to run.

   ________________________________________

   ________________________________________

6. Utha scaled and cleaned the fish so his family could eat it.

_______________________________________________

_______________________________________________

7. Asa was tired yet she climbed to the top of the mountain.

_______________________________________________

_______________________________________________

8. Guff heard the cat growling and spun around quickly.

_______________________________________________

_______________________________________________

9. Utha repaired his axe and Guff sharpened his spear.

_______________________________________________

_______________________________________________

# Task F: *Syntax Exercises*

Task F: Creating complex sentences from simple sentences, using conjunctions.

The task for this exercise is to combine short simple sentences into complex sentences. Complex sentences are connected together by coordinating conjunctions such as *after, because, before, until, since, unless, where, which, if, that, as, while,* etc. A complex sentence has a **main clause** and a **subordinate clause.** The main clause is a complete thought so is a *complete* sentence, whereas a subordinate clause *depends* on the main clause to be complete. *For instance, "Before Guff stepped in the water, he took off his boots."* The **main clause** is *"He took off his boots."* The **subordinate clause** is, *"Before Guff stepped in the water..."*

Encourage students to shorten phrases and use pronouns when needed to improve the flow of the connected sentences.

1. Guff ate the fish. He was hungry.

   Example: *Guff ate the fish* ***because*** *he was hungry.*

2. Asa wore her bearskin rug. It was cold.

   Asa ____________________because _______________.

3. Utha is a great hunter. Utha is very brave.

   Utha ____________________who _________________.

4. Guff made the fire. Guff cooked the fish.

   After ____________________he __________________

5. Guff put the shell into his pouch. The pouch was full of trinkets.

Guff ____________________ which ____________________.

6. Utha went hunting. Utha sharpened his spear.

Before ____________________ he ____________________.

7. Asa hid from the cat. The cat hunted her.

Asa ____________________ that ____________________.

9. Asa cooked the raw fish. The fish was ready to eat.

Asa ____________________ until ____________________.

10. Guff touched his dark stone. The dark stone hung around Guff's neck.

Guff ____________________ which ____________________.

# Task G: *Syntax Exercises*

Task G: *Contracting Complex Sentences*

The task for this exercise is to break down complex sentences into short simple sentences. The goal is for students to become familiar with the construction of complex sentences and note how they differ from simple and compound sentences.

1. Guff did not cross the river, because it was too deep.

   Example: *Guff did not cross the river.*

   *The river was too deep.*

2. Asa was very quiet because she was hunting rabbits.

   ________________________________________

   ________________________________________

3. While Guff was on the open plain, he was in danger.

   ________________________________________

   ________________________________________

4. Before Utha hunted for mammoth, he checked his spear for cracks.

   ________________________________________

   ________________________________________

5. As Guff scaled the cliff face, his arms became tired.

6. When it was hot, Guff loved to swim in the river.

7. It was very dangerous to approach a mammoth, unless the entire hunting party was there as a support.

8. Utha, the tribal elder, who was very brave, led the hunting party on its first great hunt of the spring.

# Task H: *Syntax Exercises*

Task H: *Expanding Sentences with Adjectives*

The task for this exercise is to expand the length of the sentence by adding an adjective to it. Adjectives also add extra detail to a character or scene. Students are encouraged to select one of the adjectives listed or choose another. Students may wish to combine several adjectives together such as '*Asa washed her hands in the **clean, clear** water.*'

1. Asa washed her hands in the water.

   Asa washed her hands in the **clear** water.

   clear clean muddy

2. Utha is a hunter.

   Utha is a ______________________________ hunter.

   cunning strong powerful

3. Guff walked in the forest.

   Guff walked in the ______________________________ forest

   dark leafy scary

4. The mammoth raised its head.

   The mammoth raised its ______________________________ head.

   massive mighty shaggy

5. Guff hunted the mammoth herd with his tribe.

Guff hunted the ________________________________herd with his tribe.

large roaming small

6. Utha collected honey from the beehive.

Utha collected ______________________________ honey from the beehive.

sweet sticky yellow

7. The old tree's branches rose high above the forest.

The old tree's branches rose high above the _____________________forest.

dry tall wet

8. The wind blew through Asa's hair.

The ________________________________ wind blew through Asa's hair.

strong fierce gentle

9. Utha ran for his life as the saber-toothed cat attacked.

Utha ran for his life as the ___________________ saber-toothed cat attacked.

ferocious angry huge

10. The wind current lifted the eagle high into the sky.

The wind current lifted the ____________________ eagle high into the sky.

beautiful graceful large

11. The lightning struck the tree and split its trunk.

The lightning struck the ____________________ tree and split its trunk.

old ancient tall

12. Guff swam in the river.

Guff swam in the ________________________________________ river.

cold warm green

13. Asa placed her toes in the river and watched as ____________________ fish swam past her feet.

silver colourful tiny

14. Guff ran up the hill.

Guff ran up the ______________________________________________ hill.

green steep wet

# Task I: *Syntax Exercises*

Task I: A*rrangement of Words to create Complete Sentences*

The goal here is to form complete and grammatically correct sentences from the jumbled sentences. The correct sentences can be found in the text, but refer to the text only when needed. A good strategy for this exercise is to cut out the words at the end of this section and move them to make different combinations until the pieces take shape and make sense as a complete sentence.

1. walked hill the tribe up

   Example: The tribe walked up the hill.

2. roared the loudly mammoth

   ________________________________________

   ________________________________________

3. morning Guff woke next the

   ________________________________________

   ________________________________________

4. mammoths long grass the ate the

   ________________________________________

   ________________________________________

5. bush behind Guff the hid

______________________________________________

______________________________________________

6. river follow to Guff decided the

______________________________________________

______________________________________________

7. rested under Guff tree old an

______________________________________________

______________________________________________

8. the water cold Guff waded into

______________________________________________

______________________________________________

9. river's walked Guff along the edge

______________________________________________

______________________________________________

10. terrible Guff in danger was

______________________________________________

______________________________________________

11. wrapped fish in Guff the leaves

______________________________________________

______________________________________________

12. Guff flames fish roasted the over

______________________________________________

______________________________________________

13. the ran tree Guff life for his to

______________________________________________

______________________________________________

# Task J: *Syntax Exercises*

Task J: *Assembling paragraphs.*

Paragraphs are a series of sentences grouped around a single main idea. In a story, a paragraph indicates particular events, setting or time, or introduces a new character or event. Students are encouraged to assemble the following individual sentences into complete paragraphs.

1. *Sentence Example:* He then carefully climbed down the cliff-face.

   Guff gripped the hard rock with his fingers.

   Guff slipped but held on to the rock.

   Guff came to a steep cliff. Guff gripped the hard rock with his fingers. He carefully climbed down the cliff-face. Guff slipped but held on to the rock. Finally, with a gentle hop, Guff landed at the bottom.

2. Sentences: The rain came down in sheets of water.

   The lightning terrified Asa.

   The thunder sounded like huge drums.

   Asa felt the storm coming before she saw it. ______________________________

   __________________________________________________________________

   ____________________________________________________________ Asa hid in the shelter.

3. Sentences: He backed away slowly.

Guff thrust his spear at the cat.

When the big cat pounced, Guff ran for his life.

The saber-toothed-cat approached Guff, snarling. ______________________

__________________________________________________________________

__________________________________________________________________

Guff climbed the tree just in time.

4. Sentences: Guff stepped into the water and felt it surge past his legs.

Guff slipped and fell into the flowing waters.

Guff was strong and able to swim across the mighty river.

The river was deep and swift but Guff needed to cross it.

__________________________________________________________________

__________________________________________________________________

__________________________________________________________________

______________________ Coughing up water, Guff made it to the opposite riverbank.

# 7

# Critical Thinking - *Problem Solving*

# Task A: *Critical Thinking Exercises*

Critical thinking is a skill that helps us when living our day to day lives. Daily we are confronted with a vast array of problems or situations that require us to make decisions. In the following exercise students need to identify *two* items to complete each task.

Task A: *Select two items needed to complete a task or solve a problem.*

1. Guff needs to climb a steep cliff. What does Guff need?

   rope fish strong boots basket

2. Utha has a broken spear handle. What does he need to repair the handle?

   rope knife bowl water

3. Asa needs to go fishing. What will she need to take?

   fishing line rug bait boots

4. Guff needs to make a fire. What will he need?

   dry wood spear flint water

5. Asa needs to cook food. What will she need?

   rug pot campfire cloak

6. Utha and Guff go hunting for mammoths. What will they need?

spear flint water blade

7. Guff hikes in the snow covered mountains. What will he need?

blade woolen cloak woolen hat spear

8. Utha wants to catch fish in a river. What will he need?

rope jug bait net

9. Utha wants to build a shelter. What will he need?

mud bricks straw spear cloak

10. A huge storm approaches. What will Guff and Asa need to protect themselves?

axe shelter roof jug

11. Utha wants to clean and scale a fish. What will he need?

rope flat dry stone blade leaves

12. Asa repairs a woolen boot. What will she need?

cloak fishing line knife string/twine

# Task B: *Critical Thinking Exercises*

Task B: *The missing piece. Complete the sequence of events.*

This exercise requires students to identify the missing piece of information.

1. Asa wants to plant a wheat seed.

   Example Sequence: Asa digs a small hole.

   She places a wheat seed in the hole.

   Asa covers the seed with soil.

   Asa sprinkles water over the spot.

2. Guff wants to climb a tree.

   Sequence: Guff places his left foot onto a low-lying branch.

   He holds a branch above his head with his left hand.

   ________________________________________

   Guff climbs to the top of the tree.

3. Utha hunts a deer.

   Sequence: Utha spots a deer a long way in the distance.

   ________________________________________

   Utha is within a spear's throw of the deer

   Utha throws his spear.

4. Guff confronts a saber-toothed cat.

Sequence: While Guff cooks fish over a fire, he hears a noise.

He turns and sees a saber-toothed cat.

_______________________________________

Guff climbs to the top of a tree.

5. Utha makes a shelter.

Sequence: Utha digs out a floor.

Utha puts up some walls.

_______________________________________

That night, Utha's family was safe and dry in the shelter when it rained.

6. Guff takes eggs from a bird nest.

Sequence: Guff started to climb the tree.

He climbed to the top of the tree and found a nest.

_______________________________________

Guff started the climb down while holding the bird eggs.

7. Asa makes a fire.

Sequence: Asa collects dry leaves and sticks.

She uses a flint to create a small flame.

________________________________________

Asa places the fish and meat over the roaring flames.

8. Utha's hunting party hunt a mammoth herd.

Sequence: The hunting party approaches the mammoth herd.

The bull mammoth senses the hunters' presence.

________________________________________

Utha runs away from the mammoth herd!

9. Guff and Asa build a raft.

Sequence: Guff cuts down a small tree.

________________________________________

Asa binds the branches with twine.

The raft is placed in the water.

# Task C: *Critical Thinking Exercises*

Task C: *Which is easier for the character to do?*

This exercise requires students to identify the relative difficulty of one situation versus the other. There is never a clear right or wrong answer. Encourage students to verbalize or write *why* they believe a particular scenario would be easier.

1. Which is *easier* for Guff to do?

   Fight a saber-toothed cat with his bare hands…

   Ride on top of a mammoth…

   ______________________________

2. Which is *easier* for Guff to do?

   Cut down a tree with a small axe…

   Make a fire with a flint and dry sticks…

   ______________________________

3. Which is *easier* for Utha to do?

   Climb to the top of a large mountain…

   Swim across a swiftly flowing river…

4. Which is *easier* for Asa to do?

Swim across a rapidly water…

Spear a fast moving fish in the flowing river…

_______________________________________________

5. Which is *easier* for Guff to do?

Steal eagle eggs from the top of a mountain…

Hunt a mammoth herd alone…

_______________________________________________

6. Which is *easier* for Asa to do?

Catch fish with a fishing line and bait…

Catch fish using a spear…

_______________________________________________

7. Which is *easier* for Utha to do?

Create a woolen tunic with an axe…

Carve a woolen tunic using a knife…

_______________________________________________

# Task D: *Critical Thinking Exercises*

Task D: *What is the problem?*

The goal for this exercise is for students to identify a potential problem for the character, based only the limited information provided. Encourage students to verbalize or write responses.

1. Guff had holes in his bearskin boots as he crossed the snow-covered mountains. *Why is this situation a potential problem for Guff?*

   ______________________________________________

2. Utha's spear broke in half as he defended himself against the saber-toothed cat. *Why is this situation a potential problem for Utha?*

   ______________________________________________

3. Guff is caught in a fierce thunderstorm a long way from any shelter.

   *Why is this situation a potential problem for Guff?*

   ______________________________________________

4. Asa still had a long way to walk back to camp and the sun was already setting.

   *Why is this situation a potential problem for Asa?*

   ______________________________________________

5. Utha was all alone on a large, flat plain when two saber-toothed cats appeared ahead. *Why is this situation a potential problem for Utha?*

______________________________________________

6. Guff lost his flint and fire lighting equipment in the middle of the harsh winter.

*Why is this situation a potential problem for Guff?*

______________________________________________

7. As Asa gathered nuts and fruit from trees, she failed to notice the large hole in her pouch. *Why is this situation a potential problem for Asa?*

______________________________________________

8. Guff was walking through a dark forest when he suddenly realized he could not tell in which direction he faced. *Why is this situation a potential problem for Guff?*

______________________________________________

9. As Utha constructed the shelter from tree branches and mud bricks, it started to rain heavily. *Why is this situation a potential problem?*

______________________________________________

10. Utha's tribe had to survive the harsh winter by hunting scarce animals in the ice and snow. *Why is this situation a potential problem for the tribe?*

______________________________________________

# Task E: *Critical Thinking Exercises*

Task E: *How to avoid the problem.*

The goal for this exercise is for students to identify potential problems and provide examples of how the character can best avoid the potential problem. Encourage students to explain their reasoning verbally or write in the space provided.

1. Guff wanted to cross the river but the water was too deep and flowing too rapidly. *To cross the river Guff could...*

   Example: Try to find a safer crossing further along the river.

2. Asa was out picking berries all day when she realized that it was getting dark and that she was far from the tribe's campsite. *Asa should have....*

   ______________________________________________

3. As Guff prepared for the hunt with his father he noticed that the spearhead was loose on the wooden shaft. *Guff should have...*

   ______________________________________________

4. Utha was just about to finish fixing his spear when he realized that he had left the twine at the last camp. He would not be able to tighten the spear. *Utha should have...*

   ______________________________________________

5. When Guff reached the safety of the camp, he remembered that he had forgotten to close his pouch. All the nuts he had gathered had fallen out. *Guff should have...*

________________________________________

6. Utha did not allow enough time to put enough straw and leaves on the roof of the shelter. That night, when it rained, Utha's family got wet. *Utha should have...*

________________________________________

7. Guff climbed the mountain peak on a misty day to see the coastline and the ocean. When he made it to the top of the mountain, he could not see much at all because of the mist. *Guff should have...*

________________________________________

8. Utha woke in the night to investigate a noise. After the search, as he walked back to the shelter, he noticed with a jolt of fear that a bear was between him and the shelter. Utha was not carrying a weapon. *Utha should have...*

________________________________________

9. When Asa reached the river after a long walk, she noticed many berries that she wished to pick. However, she had left her basket back in the camp. *Asa should have...*

________________________________________

# Task F: *Critical Thinking Exercises*

Task F: *Problem solving tough situations*

The goal for this exercise is for students to identify a difficult problem and help solve it. Encourage students to verbalize their answers or write their responses on the lines provided.

1. One day, Asa and Guff were fishing near a large lake. Without warning, a large herd of mammoth began grazing in the area. Asa and Guff, realized to their dismay that the herd of mammoths and a mighty bull mammoth were between them and their camp.

    a. Why is this a problem for Guff and Asa?

    ______________________________

    ______________________________

    b. Why would it be dangerous to try and walk *through* the herd?

    ______________________________

    ______________________________

    c. What is something Guff and Asa can do to return to their camp safely?

    ______________________________

    ______________________________

2. As Guff climbed the cliff face to collect eagle eggs from the nest, located on a rocky prominence at the top of the peak, the mother eagle spotted him with her sharp vision. With a loud squawk the great eagle swooped at Guff, her talons outstretched. Guff ducked as the eagle narrowly missed him. Guff hugged the cliff face fiercely. If he let go it now was a long drop to the bottom of the ravine, and he would not survive. Guff made himself into a small ball as the great eagle swooped once again.

a. Why is this a difficult situation for Guff?

________________________________________

________________________________________

b. Why does Guff hug the cliff face fiercely?

________________________________________

________________________________________

c. What is one thing Guff could do to improve this difficult situation?

________________________________________

________________________________________

3. Utha and the hunting party had made a mistake. The mammoths had been alerted to their presence. The hunting party had made the critical error of advancing on the herd with the wind blowing at their backs. The bull mammoth detected the hunting party's scent immediately. The massive creature confronted the tribe with its great curved tusks. All the members in the hunting party, except Utha, turned and ran. Utha stood alone with only his spear as protection as the great beast advanced toward him.

a. Why is this a problem for Utha?

________________________________________

________________________________________

b. Why did the tribe hunting party turn and run, and why did Utha stay?

________________________________________

________________________________________

c. What is something Utha can do to get out of this difficult and dangerous situation?

________________________________________

________________________________________

4. The saber-toothed cats snarled menacingly as they advanced toward Guff. Guff was trapped. At Guff's back was the edge of the cliff, and at the bottom of the cliff was the fast moving river. Guff thrust his spear, its sharp point the only thing that protected him from the big cats. He had to make a decision before the saber-toothed cats pounced.

a. Why is this a problem for Guff?

______________________________________________

______________________________________________

b. What may happen to Guff if he attempts to run past the saber-toothed cats?

______________________________________________

______________________________________________

c. What is one thing that Guff can do to escape the saber-toothed cats, even though it is dangerous?

______________________________________________

______________________________________________

5. Guff and Asa went on a foraging expedition for food. They collected a range of berries and wild vegetables, which took half the day. It was a hot day so both Guff and Asa went swimming in a nearby lake. They left the collected food supplies on a large flat rock near the lake. Later, when they returned to the rock, they discovered that forest animals had eaten all the food they had collected that day.

a. Why is this a problem for Guff and Asa?

________________________________________

________________________________________

b. What are some things that Guff and Asa could have done to protect the gathered food from animals?

________________________________________

________________________________________

c. What can Guff and Asa do about all the food that has been eaten by animals?

________________________________________

________________________________________

# 8

# Inferential Comprehension

# Inferential Comprehension

To be effective readers, and to fully understand an author's message, students need good inferencing skills. Inference skill, and by association, vocabulary knowledge, is the foundation upon which effective language and reading comprehension is built. To infer is the ability of individuals to identify missing information in written language using cognitive abilities and background knowledge. That is, students need to recall previously learnt information and use it as a foundation to evaluate *hidden* information embedded in text. Inference is a higher-level language and cognitive skill.

## Inference Example

'The mighty bull mammoth trumpeted just a few feet from where Guff lay hidden. Guff covered his ears with his hands.'

Question: Why did Guff cover his ears with his hands?

Answer: The mammoth's trumpeting was *extremely* loud and hurt Guff's ears. We can *infer* this based on both the animal's immense size and its similarity to modern elephants, which trumpet loudly to frighten any potential predators.

The questions in chapter 8 offer students the opportunity to practice thinking about hidden information in text and unlocking some of the story's deeper meanings and exploring complex themes and imagery. The questions are not just focused on the *Guff's Journey* narrative but also to the wider world that Guff lives in, and introduces new characters from Guff's tribe and offers situations to offer more variety.

# Task A: *Inference Exercises*

Task A: *Inference – Level 1*

1. When Guff heard his father calling, he stopped what he was doing, wrapped up his fishing line, put away the fish, and returned to the camp.

   What had Guff been doing?

   ______________________________

   ______________________________

2. After the rain, Asa could not relight the fire.

   Why could Asa not relight the fire?

   ______________________________

   ______________________________

3. When the tribal elder signaled to Guff to quicken his pace, Guff pointed to his foot, which was bandaged with fur skin.

   Why was Guff having difficulty keeping up?

   ______________________________

   ______________________________

4. High in the sky, the great eagles were battered by heavy winds as they struggled to maintain their altitude in the icy rain.

What was the weather like?

______________________________________________

______________________________________________

5. It fell silently throughout the night. Guff awoke in the morning to find the entire camp covered in white.

What had fallen silently throughout the night?

______________________________________________

______________________________________________

6. Mid-way through the day, Guff removed his heavy furs and had to wipe sweat from his forehead.

What type of day is it most likely to be?

______________________________________________

______________________________________________

7. Utha cut a notch at one end of the long wooden staff and jammed the chiseled stone into the notch. He then secured the stone in place with heavy twine. Utha was now ready to hunt.

What had Utha been making?

________________________________________

________________________________________

8. After a long climb, Guff finally reached the top. From up here he could see all the way to the blue water of the ocean.

Where was Guff?

________________________________________

________________________________________

9. While it was still dark, Guff, with fishing line in hand, made his way to the creek. Light was just starting to break over the horizon as he cast the line into the water.

What part of the day is it? How do you know that?

________________________________________

________________________________________

10. The light poked through the clouds and briefly bathed Asa's face with a welcome warmth.

What is the source of the light?

______________________________________________

______________________________________________

11. Guff sat down in his favorite spot and cast the line out into the flowing water. He looked across to the opposite bank and watched as a deer bent its slender neck to drink.

Where is Guff? What is he doing?

______________________________________________

______________________________________________

12. Asa whistled happily as she removed the slippery scales. She then placed the day's catch in large wet leaves. Asa then placed the leaves in the flames of the fire. The aroma wafting up from within the leaves was enticing.

What was Asa cooking?

______________________________________________

______________________________________________

# Task B: *Inference Exercises*

Task B: *Inference – Level 2*

1. Although Guff felt confident, as the tribe, with stealth, approached the mammoth herd, he felt fear in his stomach. Guff had been included in a large hunting party made up of the men of the tribe. They were hunting a mammoth herd. The tribe needed meat before the winter snows set in. The frosty ground beneath Guff's feet made a scrunching sound as he shuffled forward with little steps.

   a. Why did Guff feel "fear in his stomach" ?

   ______________________________

   ______________________________

   b. Why did the tribe approach the herd with stealth?

   ______________________________

   ______________________________

   c. Why is it important the tribe find meat before the winter snows set in?

   ______________________________

   ______________________________

   d. Why did the ground make a 'scrunching' sound?

   ______________________________

   ______________________________

2. As the first fat drops of rain started to patter down, Asa pulled in her fishing line and rushed from the river toward the camp. When she arrived at the camp, she was out of breath. She frantically helped her mother secure all the tanning animal hides and place them in the safety of the shelter. They had barely done this when the rain thundered down in sheets of driving hail, while balls of flashing light arced across the sky.

a. Why was Asa out of breath?

________________________________________

________________________________________

b. Why did the tanning hides need to be secured?

________________________________________

________________________________________

c. Why did Asa rush back to the camp?

________________________________________

________________________________________

d. What were the *balls of flashing light*?

________________________________________

________________________________________

3. Guff stood very still while the water surged strongly past his knees. He held his light, two-pronged spear high above his head. His eyes scanned the water carefully as the swift, dark forms darted between his feet. He had been standing still for some time and his teeth had begun to chatter. Suddenly, Guff's spear sliced through the water. Guff hauled the silver creature out of the water and flicked it onto the rocks near the riverbank.

a. Why was Guff standing very still?

________________________________________

________________________________________

b. What were the *swift, dark forms?*

________________________________________

________________________________________

c. Why did Guff's teeth begin to chatter?

________________________________________

________________________________________

d. What was the silver creature that Guff hauled from the water?

________________________________________

________________________________________

4. Utha took the small plank of hardwood from his bag. The wood was stained a dark brown from use. He produced another piece of wood from his bag. This wood was a medium length stick with a rounded nub on its tip. Utha carefully placed thin, dry grass on the hardwood and rubbed the tip along a shallow groove in the hardwood, near the grass. Soon, small wisps of smoke appeared. Utha gently blew on the dry grass until a tiny flame appeared.

a. What was Utha doing?

________________________________________

________________________________________

b. Had Utha often used the hardwood? How do you know this?

________________________________________

________________________________________

c. Why did Utha choose thin, dry grass?

________________________________________

________________________________________

d. Why did Utha blow gently on the dry grass?

________________________________________

________________________________________

5. The first sign of trouble was the birds all taking flight, their wings fluttering rapidly as they surged into the sky. Then Utha heard a low, threatening snarl and saw movement in the bushes to his side. Utha gripped his spear tightly, and crouched forward in a posture of defense. His muscles were tight and tense as if carved from wood. Utha's eyes glinted as the great feline emerged from the bushes. The huge upper jaw of the great beast opened to reveal long curved teeth. Utha was ready.

a. Why did the birds suddenly take flight?

________________________________________

________________________________________

b. What caused the movement in the bushes?

________________________________________

________________________________________

c. Why did Utha's muscles feel as if carved from wood?

________________________________________

________________________________________

d. What could the great feline be?

________________________________________

________________________________________

# 9

# Shared Reading Strategies

# Strategic Reading and Language Comprehension

The goal of shared strategic reading, or context based language comprehension intervention, is not to teach students how to decode. The principal goal of shared strategic reading is to target students' language and meta-linguistic awareness skills. The ultimate goal is for students with language and comprehension difficulty to independently recognize and repair their own comprehension breakdowns.

## Scaffolding through Linguistic Facilitation

Scaffolding is a term borrowed from the construction industry. In the construction industry, scaffolding is used to provide a temporary support structure for workers and tools as the building is being constructed or repaired. As the building takes shape, it eventually reaches a stage where it can stand unaided. The scaffolding is then gradually removed. Similarly, instructional scaffolding, as used with linguistic facilitation, is a series of structured oral language strategies and tools that teachers and clinicians use to support students' language and reading comprehension. The goal is for instructional scaffolding to be gradually removed as students attain a level of competence and mastery in identifying their own comprehension breakdowns.

Skilled readers are actively involved in the understanding of difficult text. When proficient readers read a passage that they have not understood, they may reread the passage - sometimes several times - to ensure they have understood the meaning. This is especially true of highly complex text. In contrast, readers with poor comprehension skills often don't recognize when they have not clearly understood a passage. Such readers will simply continue reading not realizing they have missed a large chunk of meaning that may be essential to understanding a book or story as a whole. Students who do not or cannot repair their comprehension failure will need to be explicitly taught language comprehension repair skills. One of the most effective means of teaching comprehension repair strategies is to scaffold comprehension breakdown using a variety of linguistic facilitation techniques.

# Linguistic Facilitation Techniques

Effective language intervention are structured and prompt students to think about difficult text in a reflective way. As teachers of oral language, educators and speech clinicians support students' understanding of difficult text through a range of scaffolded facilitation techniques. This section features effective oral and written language techniques in the form of graphic organizers that are used to scaffold targeted language behaviour to improve students' reading and language comprehension.

## Preparatory Sets

Building background knowledge prior to reading a text is achieved using preparatory sets. These are used to trigger students' background knowledge about a particular topic. Students with reading comprehension problems have difficulty understanding text, often because of poor vocabularies and impoverished semantic word knowledge. Preparatory sets focus students' attention on target words or themes. This extra focus creates an expectation of the text passage's probable meaning.

## Semantic Map

Semantic maps are tools that are often used in conjunction with preparatory sets. Semantic maps are used to brainstorm information about a particular word or topic. They are useful in building a detailed amount of background knowledge.

## Extensions

The clinician or teacher comments about a selected passage to expand on a target or specific aspect of the text. The teacher's role is to model insights about the text and invite students to add their own interpretation. Extensions are a vital and important tool that can greatly expand a student's understanding of a particular passage. Extensions work by adding *meaning* to unfamiliar words and phrases.

# Expansions

When we expand a student's utterance, we provide grammatical and syntactical details to it that supports the student's words so that they more resemble adult language forms. For example, if a child says, '*bike go fast,*' we can expand the utterance with, '*Yes, the bike goes fast. The bike is going fast,*' etc.

# Imitations

Imitations are a valuable tool that involve the clinician simply repeating what the student has said. By repeating the student's utterances, we increase the amount of times the student produces lexical, syntax and morphological forms.

# Immersion

Immersion provides a high number of the target concept in different but related forms while interacting in a game, reading a book or any other language activity. By the clinician immersing students in language where the target form is repeatedly provided, students will be prompted to attempt the new form in their own communication. For example, the clinician wishes to teach the concepts of *harmony* while focusing on the target text passage. **Clinician**: *'Let's have a look at the word harmony. Harmony is something which is consistent and pleasing. Like a harmony in a song, or a harmony in an orchestra. People can also be in harmony if they work well together in a consistent way. So they work harmoniously'* etc.

# Cloze Procedures

Cloze procedures use the context of a situation to assist students to identify a word they find difficult to say, or have yet to attempt. Students are prompted to fill in the blank or gap in a sentence or phrase. For instance, **Clinician**: *'Another word for feline is c......'* The clinician produces only the first phoneme. The student is prompted to say '*cat.*'.

# Paraphrasing

Paraphrasing is used to define a difficult word or reword a complex sentence into shorter simpler sentences. In doing this you effectively help to reduce the complexity of a passage and increase students' understanding of a section of text. The following example illustrates this point. The clinician reads from the text, 'As Guff scanned the immense scene, he felt small, like an ant standing upon a seemingly infinite, newly cured and stretched skin of a great mammoth.' **Clinician**: *'That's a long sentence. Let's see if we can break the down a little. Guff is looking at large mountains that stretch to the horizon. We can imagine how it might feel to be a tiny ant standing on an immense rug. It might look like the rug would never end. The sentence features the word,* ***infinite****, which means to go on forever. So we can imagine that Guff is surrounded by big mountains, and he feels very small'* etc.

# Generalization

Generalization is an effective language arts tool that links events and themes from a story passage to events or situations that the student may have experienced in their own life. Generalizations increase a student's understanding and comprehension of new information by making an association with information they already know. For example, **Clinician**: *'Have you ever been to the mountains or gone skiing? You have? That's great. Well think about how large and scary those mountains are. How do you think it would feel to be lost, alone in the mountains?'*

# Summarization

Summarization is an essential component of language arts. In summarization, the clinician restates the ideas discussed during the session and the information learnt just before the session ends. All sessions should be summarized to help students with language comprehension difficulties remember complex information.

# Graphic Organizers

A graphic organizer is defined as a graphic representation of all or part of the elements of a particular concept you wish to teach. Graphic organizers are a popular technique to facilitate comprehension because they encourage organized thought and are an excellent *visual aid* when learning complex information. This book uses a number of graphic organizers which are central to a shared strategic reading when teaching language concepts. The graphic featured in this chapter organizers can be found in **Appendix** C.

The **pre-story background** graphic organizer is used by the clinician to high-light features of a story so as to provide appropriate back-ground knowledge for students. Students will also be able link any new information encountered in the story to ideas previously explored in the pre-story back-ground graphic organizer.

Pre-Story Background Map

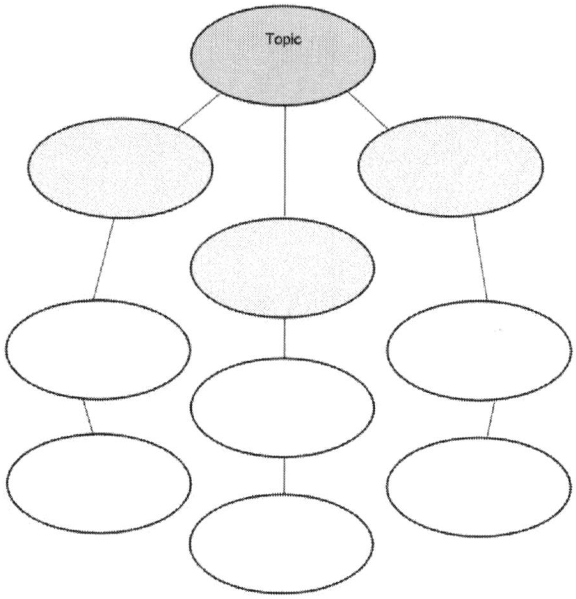

# Graphic Organizers

The **semantic map – nouns** graphic organizer is effective at exploring the different aspects of a noun whether it be an object or animal or a proper noun such as a person or a specific place.

Semantic Map for Nouns

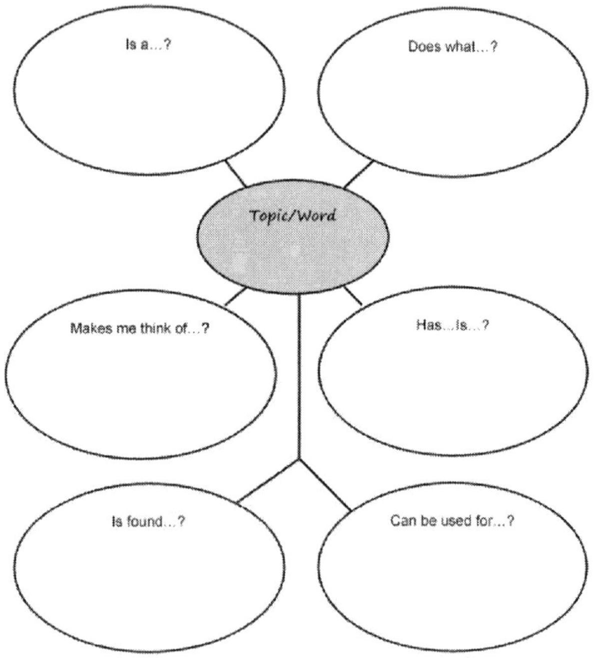


Similarly to the **semantic map – nouns** graphic organizer, the adjectives map helps explore multiple characteristics of adjectives, including possible synonyms and antonyms.

Semantic Map for Adjectives

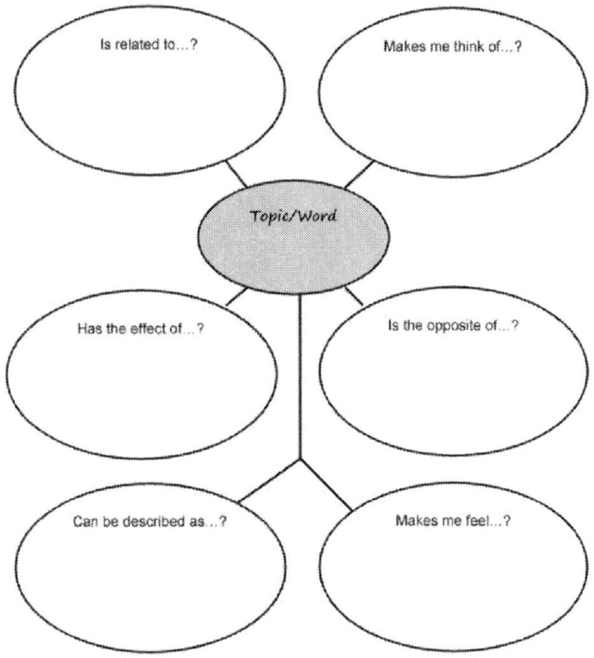

# Graphic Organizers

The **vocabulary map** graphic organizer is great for exploring synonyms and antonyms of a target word or words. A feature of this graphic organizer is replacing a word or phrase from the author's original text to discuss the author's choice of a particular word or phrase.

Vocabulary Map

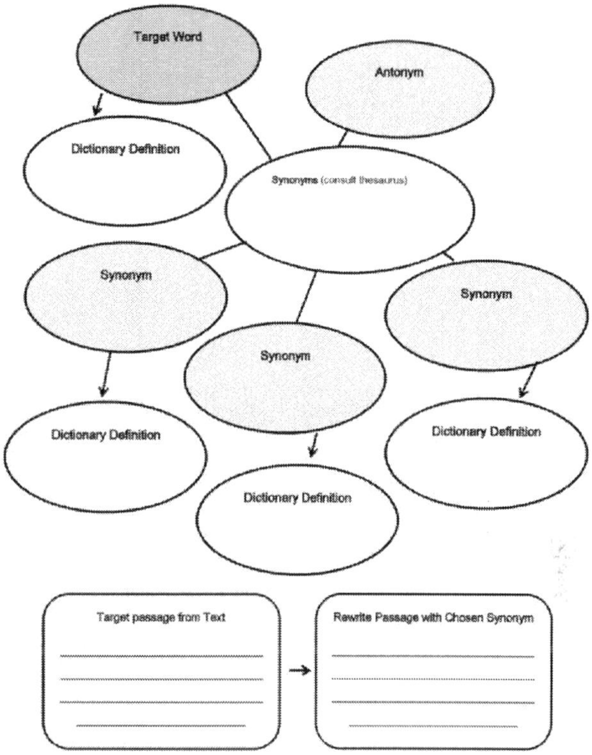

# Graphic Organizers

The **story grammar map** graphic organizer explores the fundamental structure of a story and the sequence of events within the story structure.

### Story Grammar Map

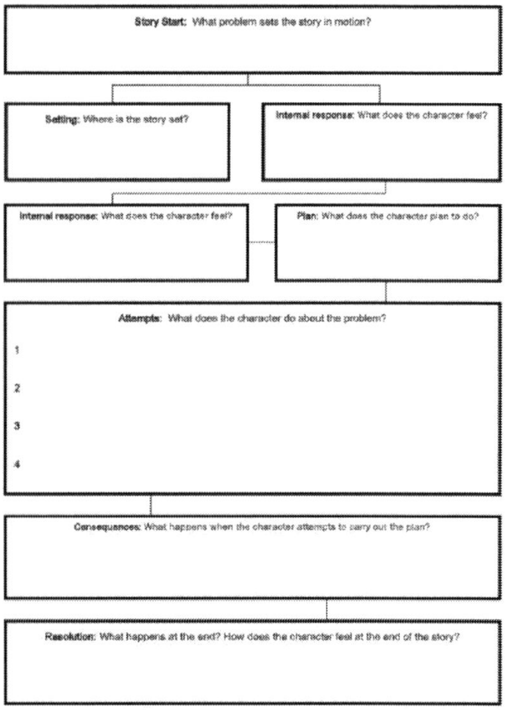

Story Start: What problem sets the story in motion?
Setting: Where is the story set?
Internal response: What does the character feel?
Internal response: What does the character feel?
Plan: What does the character plan to do?
Attempts: What does the character do about the problem?
1
2
3
4
Consequances: What happens when the character attempts to carry out the plan?
Resolution: What happens at the end? How does the character feel at the end of the story?


The **story grammar character map** graphic organizer explores the myriad details that make up a character in a storybook. Several characters can be explored at once with the story grammar character map.

### Story Grammar Character Map

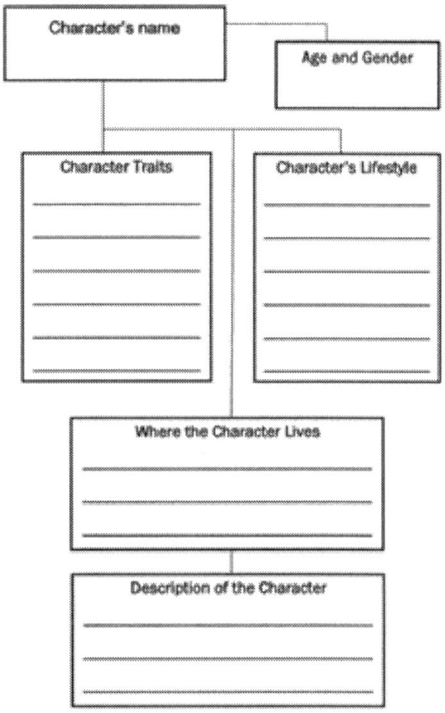

# Communicative Reading Strategies Guide 1

**Passage from Text:** 'The storm tossed the tiny boat on the seas as if it were a matchstick. The sun shone for a moment, but its warming rays were quickly engulfed by the angry and bruised sky.'

**Preparatory Set** *(Background knowledge)*

Assists the reader to recall background knowledge about the text passage.

**Example:** *"What usually happens in a storm? A storm affects the sea by making the waves get bigger.* etc... (Use a **semantic map** to explore different aspects of 'storm.')

### Semantic Map

Graphic organizers provide a visual representation of linguistic concepts and the relationship between different aspects of language.

### Paraphrasing

Paraphrasing is used to reword text. It can be used to define a difficult word or reword a complex sentence into shorter simpler sentences.

**Example: Text** – 'The sun shone for a moment, but its warming rays were quickly engulfed by the angry and bruised sky.' **Clinician:** *'It sounds like the sun shone through the clouds. So while it was able to shine it provided some warmth. It didn't last very long though. The angry and stormy sky enveloped the sun's rays again.'*

### Questioning

**Fact Based Question:** A question that has a specific answer. *'What did the sun do?'*

**Surface level Inference Question:** Questions that asks about something that is hinted at in the text. *'What would a bruised and angry sky look like?*

**Deep level Inference Question:** Questions which do not rely on textual information. *'Will the boat and its crew survive? How do you know?'*

### Parsing

Parsing comes from the Latin word meaning *part*. When parsing, you **chunk** something into separate parts. Parsing helps students to understand that a sentence is made up of **separate** units.

**Example from text:** 'The storm tossed the tiny boat...' *'Find out what the storm did.'* **(Point to word 'tossed')** *'Tossed' is a past tense verb.*

### Generalization

Link the events from the story to real life events from the student's own experiences.

**Example:** *'Have you ever been on a boat in rough seas, or got caught in a storm?'*

### Summarization

The student, guided by the clinician, recounts the events in the story passage they have discussed. The clinician provides a summary of the session and the themes discussed during the session.

# Communicative Reading Strategies Guide 2

Passage from Text: 'The storm tossed the tiny boat on the seas as if it were a matchstick. The sun shone for a moment, but its warming rays were quickly engulfed by the angry and bruised sky.'

### Association

This technique creates links between an idea and/or sentence currently being read and information that has previously been read. Association helps the reader make links between different passages, which helps in understanding story cohesion and sequence.

**Example: Clinician:** *'The sky was **angry and bruised**, which is perhaps what the sky might look like in a **storm**.'* **(Links to first sentence in passage)**

### Cloze Procedure

Cloze procedures are a highly useful tool that uses story context to assist a student to identify a word they find difficult to decode. The student is required to fill in the blank or gap in a sentence.

**Example: Clinician:** *'The sun...(pause) for a moment.'*

**Student:** *'The sun...**shone...**for a moment.'*

### Acknowledgement

Acknowledgement is a technique that the clinician uses to confirm to the reader that what they have read has been understood by both reader and facilitator. It is used to demonstrate that reading is a natural part of communication

**Example: (Student reads text)** *'The storm tossed the tiny boat on the seas as if it were a matchstick.'* **Clinician:** *'Wow, the storm must have been fierce if the boat seemed to be as little as a matchstick.'*

### Choice or Contrast Questions

Provide choice and contrast questions if a student has difficulty understanding the meaning of a particular word or passage. Give the student some choices to think with and some contrast within those choices.

**Example: Clinician:** *'The waves made the boat seem as if it were the size of a matchstick. Were the waves very large or quite small?'*

### Cloze Procedure with Gesture

**Example: Clinician:** *'The sun... **(Gesture as if sun's rays are spreading out – 'shine-shone')**...for a moment.'*

### Cloze Procedure with Phonemic Cue

**Example: Clinician:** *'The sun /sh/ ... for a moment.'*

**Student:** *'The sun sh**one...**'*

### Semantic Cue

A semantic cue is useful when a student has difficulty recognizing a word or is confronted with a new word they find difficult to decode. Use a dictionary to find the word's meaning and a thesaurus to find the synonym.

**Example: Clinician:** *'The word "**engulf**" means to be swallowed up or overwhelmed.' I think that's a clever way of describing the scene.' Let's have a look at the dictionary...'*

# 10

# Shared Reading Intervention

# Shared Reading Intervention - Introduction

The informal assessment of our fictional student Daniel's oral narrative retell and inferential comprehension in chapter 2 revealed that Daniel has difficulty with aspects of oral and written language, particularly semantic word use and inference ability. Semantic word knowledge and inferential comprehension have thus been chosen as appropriate targets for language intervention.

This chapter details shared reading contextualized language intervention with examples of the clinician shaping and helping to construct Daniel's responses. The goal of intervention is to promote Daniel's understanding of the text and model and influence his verbal responses. Intervention is focused on unlocking *Guff's Journey* deeper themes and to stimulate more complex expressive language from Daniel.

As stated in the introductory pages, shared reading is a powerful means of utilizing the context of a familiar story to prompt students to think about language on a metalinguistic or conscious level. This clinician-directed intervention method ultimately improves students' comprehension of text and teaches and promotes a conscious and close reading of complex stories.

## Shared Reading Intervention – *Guff's Journey*

**Objectives:** The clinician's goals include assisting Daniel to manage some of the complexities of the *Guff's Journey* story, develop effective comprehension strategies using graphic organizers and increase his expressive vocabulary. The clinician will use metalinguistic awareness to facilitate Daniel's understanding of the text.

**Learning Approach:** Communicative Reading Strategies and scaffolded language stimulation.

**Materials:** Guff's Journey story, graphic organizer worksheets, dictionary, thesaurus, small portable whiteboard, markers

**Rating System:** Semantic Word Knowledge rating chart and Inference Knowledge chart

# Shared Reading Session - Introduction

For this session the clinician has targeted a passage close to the beginning of the *Guff's Journey* story. Daniel had some initial difficulty on his first reading of this particular passage with several words and concepts proving to be challenging. Several of the words that Daniel had specific difficulty with have been highlighted, while the sentences and phrases italicized are targets for inferential comprehension.

# Passage from *Guff's Journey* Story

'Guff sensed something enormous shadow him. He felt the rhythmic crunch of its legs impact the ground just behind him, its breath a series of loud bursts. Soon it would crush him. Guff's chest was a torment from fatigue as he strained to keep running. In his panic, Guff failed to see that the ground had suddenly vanished from under him. He shrieked and fell into blackness down a steep hill.' (Excerpt from Scene 2, *Guff's Journey*)

# Shared Reading – Vocabulary Intervention

The clinician has previously worked with Daniel on the **Prestory Background** section in chapter 4. Thus before the session begins, Daniel has a basic knowledge of Guff as a character and a rudimentary understanding of the world that Guff inhabits. The clinician sits across from Daniel and begins the session by reading through the target passage once more with Daniel. The target words are highlighted. The target words for the session are *torment, rhythmic,* and *impact.* The target words are typically words that a student may have had exposure to from other text, but not necessarily understand their meaning. The words *torment, rhythmic* and *torment* will need to be taught explicitly using the context of the story to scaffold their meaning. The clinician has several copies of Semantic Maps for Nouns and Vocabulary Maps printed for the word learning session.

**Clinician**: 'Some of the words from this passage are a little tricky. I would like to explore them in more detail.'

The clinician places the **Semantic Map for Nouns** before the student. The clinician writes the word *torment* into the dark shaded word/topic box.

**Clinician**: 'It says here that Guff ran and that he ran even though his chest was a *torment.* What do you think the word *torment* means in this context? Are you familiar with the word *torment*?'

**Daniel**: 'I'm not sure. I don't know what it means.'

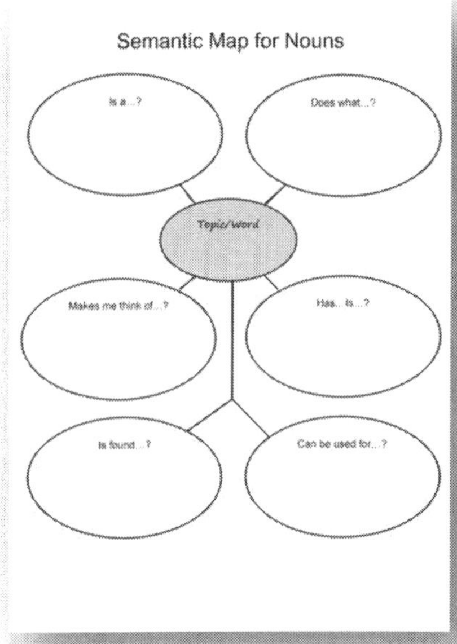


**Clinician**: 'When I find a word in books I don't know I usually look up the word in a dictionary. Let's look up the word *torment* in the dictionary.'

Daniel looks up the word in the dictionary using the **dictionary guide** which provides a helpful structure for Daniel to quicken the search for the word *torment*. Daniel is encouraged by the clinician to read the definition.

**Daniel**: 'Torment is something which causes mental or physical pain.'

**Clinician**: 'That's right. It says in the text that Guff's chest is a **torment**. Do you think he might be in pain as he runs?'

**Daniel**: 'Yes.'

**Clinician**: 'Yes I believe he is in some pain. His legs are also cramping. You may have run a lot while playing sport and found it hard to breathe or your legs become really sore from running.

The clinician uses a number of shared reading strategies to extend Daniel' understanding of the word *torment* within the context of the *Guff's Journey* story using **extension**, **generalization** and **association**.

**Clinician**: 'Guff's chest was a **torment** as he ran which tells us that his heart and lungs must have been straining. So he certainly felt the physical **torment** of running, but we can also infer that he must have felt the emotional **torment** as well. Imagine having a massive animal chasing you. Also, Guff is separated from his father and tribe. It must be terrifying for Guff, both here in this scene and later in the rest of the story. Remember, **torment** relates to both physical and mental pain.'

Daniel is then encouraged by the clinician to fill in the **Semantic Map for Nouns** worksheet for the word *torment*. With some scaffolding provided, Daniel completes the semantic map. Note that not every box is applicable to the word *torment*.

- Does what... — *Not applicable*
- Has...Is... — Is a form of physical or emotional pain
- Can be used to... — *Not applicable*
- Is found... — In this context *torment* relates to Guff's chest and breathing pain and fatigue
- Makes me think of... — Times when I've been exhausted while running
- Is related to... — Discomfort, fatigue, exhaustion

The clinician provides a quick summary of the meaning of the word *torment* in the context of the target passage before moving to the next target word, *impact*.

**Clinician**: 'We've learnt so far that *torment* relates to physical pain and emotional pain. Guff must feel a lot of pain in his chest because he is running so fast, which must be exhausting for Guff. We both know how it feels to have trouble being out of breath after we've run in a race. I want to now explore two other words from this passage, *rhythmic* and *impact*. We'll start with the word *impact*.'

The clinician introduces the next target word, *impact*. Note that impact in the context of the story is a verb. The **Semantic Map for Adjectives** can be used to explore adjectives as well as some verbs.

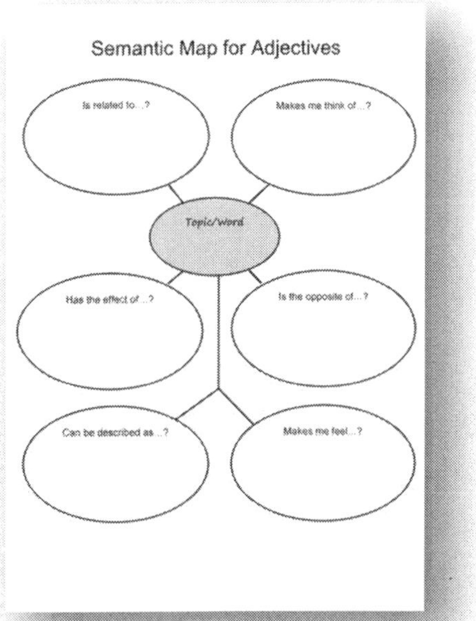


The clinician places the **Semantic Map for Adjectives** before the student. The clinician writes the word *impact* into the dark shaded word/topic box.

**Clinician**: 'This is a semantic map for adjectives, but *impact* is not an adjective; it is in fact a verb. The word *impact* can also be a noun. In our story it states that *the crunch of its legs impact the ground.* The legs *impact* the ground. *Impact* is a verb in the context of this passage. Do you know what *impact* means?'

**Daniel**: 'No.'

**Clinician**: 'The same as we did before with the word *torment*, let's search for i*mpact* in the dictionary.'

Daniel once again uses the dictionary and **dictionary guide** to search for the word *impact*. Daniel is encouraged by the clinician to read the definition.

**Daniel**: 'If you *impact* something you drive it into the ground with considerable force.'

**Clinician**: 'What do you think is driving into the ground with great force just behind Guff as he runs. Use the picture to help you if needed.

**Daniel**: 'The mammoth's legs?'

**Clinician**: 'I agree. The mammoth is just behind Guff as he runs for his life. The mammoth's legs strike the ground with such force that they *impact* the ground. **Impact** refers to considerable force or lots of force. Why do you think the mammoth's legs **impact**?'

**Daniel**: 'Because the mammoth has big legs and it's heavy.'

The clinician uses communicative reading strategies once again to extend Daniel's understanding of the target word, *impact*. The clinician uses **extension**, **paraphrasing** and **semantic cues**.

**Clinician**: 'Yes, that's right. Well done. A mammoth, especially the bull mammoth, is a huge and very heavy animal and his legs *impact* on the ground just behind Guff due to the animal's massive size. The thing that followed Guff as being as big as a mountain. It surely must have felt like that to Guff to be pursued by such a massive animal.'

Daniel is then encouraged by the clinician to fill in the **Semantic Map for Adjectives** worksheet for the word *impact*. With some scaffolding provided, Daniel completes the semantic map. Note that not every box is applicable for the word *impact*.

- Makes me think of… heavy, pounding, crunch
- Is the opposite of… stillness, quiet
- Makes me feel… scared for Guff
- Can be described as… heavy sound
- Has the effect of… crushing, pounding
- Is related to… crunching, pounding, heavy

As before with the word *torment*, the clinician provides a quick summary of the meaning of the word *impact* in the context of the target passage.

**Clinician**: 'We've learnt that *torment* relates to physical and emotional pain. Guff must feel a lot of physical pain in his chest because he is running so fast which must be exhausting. We know how it feels to have trouble breathing when we've run in a race. We have also learnt that *impact* can be a verb and is something which drives into the ground with considerable force. The mammoth's legs are so massive and heavy that the impact of its legs striking the ground would be quite powerful.'

The clinician next places a copy of the **Semantic Map for Adjectives** before the student. The clinician prepares to move attention on to the final word to be discussed for this session, the word *rhythmic*.

Once again, the clinician uses shared reading strategies to broaden and develop Daniel's understanding of the target word, *rhythmic.* The clinician uses **extension, generalization** and **paraphrasing** and completes the session with a **summarization.** The clinician initially prompts Daniel to look up the word *rhythmic* in the dictionary. Daniel does require some assistance due to the complexity of the dictionary definition.

Dictionary definitions of words do not always provide a user-friendly representation of a word's meaning written as they are in such formal language. However, definitions do provide a useful starting point for clinician-directed discussion on the word's meaning within a particular context.

**Daniel:** '*Rhythmic* means something which recurs with measured regularity.'

**Clinician:** 'Yes, so the dictionary definition mentions regular and measured. That reminds me of our heart. You see the heart is always regular and measured. Heart beats are always the same beat, always regular and always measured. Same as when we walk. Our walking is regular and measured. It's always the same: one measured step in front of the other. In the text it states, *Guff felt the rhythmic crunch of its legs impact the ground behind him.* So we can infer that the mammoth's steps were the same in that they were *rhythmic,* measured and regular. So in this context the rhythmic crunch of the mammoth's legs striking the earth would have sounded like *crunch... crunch...crunch...crunch* with the exact same amount of time between each crunch. We know this because the crunches were described as *rhythmic* and we know that *rhythmic* indicates a regular and measured beat or time.'

Daniel is then encouraged by the clinician to fill in the **Semantic Map for Adjectives** worksheet for the word *rhythmic.* With some scaffolding provided, Daniel completes the semantic map. Note that not every box is applicable to the word *rhythmic.*

- Makes me think of... regular, steady, measured
- Is the opposite of... irregular, unsteady
- Makes me feel... the same beat, like a beating heart
- Can be described as... always the same, steady
- Has the effect of... same rhythm, like a metronome
- Is related to... ticking clock, steady walk, beating heart

The clinician completes the vocabulary intervention session by **summarizing** the words that were covered in the session, once again placing the words in the context of the *Guff's Journey* story.

**Clinician**: 'Today we have covered three words and learnt about the meaning of the words within the context of the *Guff's Journey* story. The words we have learnt are *torment, impact* and *rhythmic*. We learnt that *torment* is related to pain or exhaustion, *impact* is a verb that means to drive into the ground with great force and *rhythmic* is a regular and measured beat.

## Using the Vocabulary Rating Chart

The clinician writes the three words into the rating chart boxes. The clinician assigns each word a score of 1 due to Daniel having had only an initial exposure to the three words. The words will need to be taught again several times before true mastery of the words is achieved.

### Vocabulary Knowledge Rating Chart

The rating chart measures a student's understanding of a target concept. The rating system is subjective in manner but provides a convenient and relatively accurate measure of a student's competence with a newly learnt concept or word.

| Score | Description | | |
|---|---|---|---|
| Score the student's response/s, as best can be determined, in the appropriate column | 0. The student has no real understanding of the target word or concept.<br>1. The student has some understanding of the target word or concept, but has trouble describing it or writing it.<br>2. The student has good knowledge of the target word or concept and can describe it and write it well when prompted.<br>3. The student has very good understanding of the target word or concept and uses it correctly in context, written and verbal. | | |
| | Word/Concept | Word/Concept | Word/Concept |
| | torment | impact | rhythmic |
| Date 17/09/2015 | Score 1 | Score 1 | Score 1 |

## Vocabulary Map Completion – Additional Activity Option

The clinician completed a vocabulary map with the student to focus more attention on a single word. In this case the word *torment* was selected for further discussion and exploration and the circular boxes completed.

## Vocabulary Map

**Target passage from Text**

Guff's chest was a *torment* from fatigue as he strained to keep running.

→

**Target passage from Text - Rewrite**

Guff's chest was *in distress* from fatigue as he strained to keep running.

## Suggested Target Words for Vocabulary Intervention

Below is the *Guff's Journey* text and some suggested words to target for vocabulary intervention. The wordlist, though not exhaustive, provides a starting point for selection of words to begin vocabulary intervention. The suggested high utility words are highlighted in grey.

**Scene 1**

The dry grass pressed fierce into Guff's legs as he lay in the dirt, but he did not complain. Guff was on his first hunt with the elders and he needed to be quiet as a field mouse. Above the hunters loomed a mighty bull muloth, its tusks curved and lethal. Sweat beaded Guff's forehead though the day was cold. Guff's father, Utha, anxious for Guff, searched his eyes and then smiled. Utha's arm muscles were tense and corded as if carved from oak. He lay flat beside other men of the tribe a short spear toss from Guff. Between the tribe's spears and fat calves was the bull.

Guff's heart flipped like a fish when the bull mammoth suddenly stomped close to where he lay. The brute had located a rich cluster of long grass that unhappily was just above Guff's head. The snort of the giant's breath rippled Guff's hair, while the stink of its shaggy mane filled his nostrils. The muloth tore out chunks of grass and crushed it in its jaws. Another mouthful and Guff's cover would be gone. Guff's hands trembled as he gripped his stone-tipped spear. He could not breathe well. This was happening too fast. His heart thumped like a leather drum beaten with a stick. The pounding was so loud in Guff's ears that he was certain the bull would hear.

**Scene 2**

What happened next were swift, fleeting actions and blasts of noise - men shouting and the furious peal and roar of the muloths. Spears buzzed through the air like insects. Guff stood though had no memory of getting to his feet. Something big hit him in the side and he soared through the air, weightless. The next instant the air was ripped from his chest when he struck the hard dirt. The big sky whirled. He could hear Utha above the confusion, howling, *'Guff, Guff'*. He tried to call to his father but his mouth failed to form the words. Guff scrambled to his feet as blood surged to his head. His thoughts were jumbled, so he ran. His father and tribe were gone, scattered. Guff sensed something enormous shadow him. He felt the rhythmic crunch of its hooves impact the ground just behind him, its breath a series of loud bursts. Soon it would crush him. Guff's chest was a torment from fatigue as he strained to keep running. In his panic, Guff failed to see that the ground had suddenly vanished from under him. He shrieked and fell into blackness down a steep hill.

Much later, Guff slowly opened his eyes and winced. Sunlight trickled in. His thoughts were murky. He could make out shadows and shapes and saw that the sun was about to leave the big sky. The mammoth was gone. The half-light before dark crept with long fingers across the land. Guff's fogginess cleared. He saw for the first time that he lay in a ditch. His back ached but he could move his limbs. His spear lay beside him, undamaged. Guff's stone blade, wrapped in its leather pouch, was still attached to his leggings. His father would be pleased. He slowly poked his head above the ditch. He was in a deep ravine. Mountains rose sharp and pitiless on all sides. In the half-light, the peaks were cold, vast and glowing. The last wisps of gold and warmth clung to the tops of the harsh crests. Too soon, the threads of light faded to nothing and the evening gloom deepened. Guff was alone in the dark for the first time in his life.

**Scene 3**

Guff huddled and shivered beneath the great night orb. His father's words bounced in his head. *"If lost at night. Make no sound. Be not seen nor heard."* Guff was indeed lost. The search for his tribe would begin with first light, but first he had to survive the night. Guff wrapped himself in his furs but the cold defeated him. He stayed awake through the long dark, fearful of making the smallest sound as night animals hunted. He prayed silently to his ancestors while his ears strained for sounds of great beasts; the throaty snort of the great bear, the piercing roar of the monster with teeth like long blades.

The dawn found Guff with his head buried within his cloak, ice in his hair. Short puffs of mist escaped from his mouth. When the sun rose above the sharp peaks, Guff felt joy. Despite his aching back, he had faith that he would find his father today. Guff lifted himself from the ditch and walked to the river at the bottom of the ravine. He scooped water in his hands and drank for a long time. He was terribly thirsty and the water was cold and delicious. Guff could feel strength return, the panic of the previous day wash away. He gripped his spear and began to trot across large flat stones that warmed in the morning sun. Guff's father had said that when lost, a river could lead you home. Guff's people could be camped on the banks of this river.

**Scene 4**

Guff followed the curve of the river. His leg throbbed which slowed his pace as he watched for beasts that may be at the water's edge. Apart from a few otters, with eyes like black pebbles, Guff saw nothing. Later that morning, Guff climbed to the top of a cliff that blocked his path and saw much that frightened him. Mountains stretched out to a vast distance, all the way to the big sky. Guff felt like an ant standing upon a newly cured and stretched skin of a muloth. Guff climbed back down into the ravine and once again followed the snake-like river. He trotted along the river's edge until the mist had left the valley. The sun was directly above Guff when he reached the shore of a large lake. He hoped that the river continued again further down. The lake's surface was calm. Mountain peaks reflected in the lake's icy water and a thin vapor whispered up from the water's surface. The sight of the lake was soothing. Guff's breath was ragged from fatigue and his injured leg throbbed He was hungry and had not eaten for days.

Guff felt he needed to keep moving but he was also very tired. He sat near the lake's surface to rest. His eyes scanned the banks of the lake for movement, but the area was quiet. No bears, no big cats. Near to where Guff rested, were the bones of an elk. It had lain there a long time for the bones were clean and bleached white. Guff lay his head upon a flat stone and closed his eyes.

**Scene 5**

Guff awoke to the sound of tiny splashes, like flat stones skipped across water. He tracked the sound and glimpsed darting fish breach the lake's surface to feed on insects. Guff needed a fishing spear, a water spear. He walked slowly to the elk bones; nursing his sore leg. Guff picked out rib bones. These he honed and carved with his blade so that both ends were sharp. Guff cut the bindings of his spear and removed the stone spear tip. He cut new notches into the spear's shaft and attached the newly sculpted rib bones to the wood. Guff then shaped and slotted the bones neatly into the grooves and bound the bones with twine. The spear now featured spikes of sharp bone.

Guff stepped into the bitterly cold water and raised his spear. He balanced and waited, careful not to move. The water nipped his legs, like sharp teeth piercing his skin. He could not stand in this water for long. Guff scanned the surface of the lake for movement. Suddenly, a hint of fin stabbed the surface close to where he stood. Guff launched the spear. Guided by luck, mostly, and some skill it sliced into the flesh of a fish the size of his forearm. Guff hauled the fish into the air and droplets of water sprinkled in his hair. He whooped with excitement and flicked the spear. The fish landed flapping on big stones near the water's edge, its scales glistening in the sun. Guff was relieved to haul his legs from the frigid water. His teeth chattered as he struck the fish's head with a rock. He then removed its scales with his blade. By the time Guff had finished preparing the fish, the sun was low in the sky and the shadows were long. He would travel no further today. Guff did not wish to sleep huddled in the cold this night chewing raw fish. He knew the dangers, but he would cook the fish.

**Scene 6**

Guff gathered leaves, bark and branches from the base of an old tree. He possessed a dark stone that hung safe from his neck, stuck to leather twine by pitch. The stone was sharp and shaped like a leaf. The stone's value was greater than his spear or blade; the stone made fire. Guff selected a flat rock and placed dried grass on it. He struck the rock with the dark stone. The stone struck at an angle so that sparks landed in the tufts of dry grass. After some effort, a wisp of smoke appeared. Guff blew on the twist of smoke until a flame stretched and curled. Excited, he layered more grass and thin strips of bark on the tiny flame until it grew. Guff skewered the fish onto a sharpened stick and wrapped it in green leaves from a nearby water plant. He then roasted the fish over the flames. Its aroma made his stomach rumble. Guff removed the fish from the flames, unwrapped the now blackened leaves and picked the flesh from the fish's bones. The flesh was hot and singed Guff's fingers, but it was delicious - charred on the outside, sweet in the middle.

Guff finished eating and threw a large branch on the fire. He watched sleepily as sparks and smoke climbed into the twilight air.

**Scene 7**

A shadow loomed. Guff could only sense the shadow's dark outline he felt a spike of pure fear that pierced his heart. The beast prowled slowly, sniffing the air, tracing Guff's scent through the smoke. The creature's head took shape beyond the shroud of smoke. The beast opened its jaws to reveal terrible long teeth. Guff felt the blood drain from his face. Here was death, a short stone toss from where he sat. If Guff moved too quickly, the beast would see him instantly. Guff never took his eyes off the monster as he slowly sorted his limbs and silently prepared his spear. Guff realized to his dismay that the spear was now only useful for stabbing fish.

Guff's only chance was to reach the old tree. He gave a short prayer to his ancestors and leapt to his feet. Guff then threw the spear at the beast with all his strength. The spear flew true and struck the side of the great cat, just below its shoulder. The force caused the bones bound to the spear to break and scatter like a dandelion seed in a gust of wind. The spear failed to pierce the beast's thick hide. But for a moment, the big cat was off balance. It snarled. Its ears flat against its head. It saw Guff and its yellow eyes narrowed, its muscles tensing. The beast roared and leapt.

Guff lunged for the tree. In a few strides, he reached the base of the tree. He grasped blindly at the branches above his head. Guff's fingers gripped thick bark and he frantically pulled himself up. An instant later, the tree shuddered as the heavy animal slammed into it. But Guff was just out of reach and the beast could only bellow in frustration. It lurked at the tree's base and stared up at Guff with its fierce eyes.

In the distance, Guff could hear voices, his name called. His name, the most beautiful sound in the world. Startled, the big cat bounded away. Guff looked down through the branches and saw his father and other men from their tribe sprinting to the tree. They had been tracking Guff and had seen the smoke from his fire. A wave of emotion like clear water washed through Guff. He climbed down from the tree and was embraced by his father.

# 11

# Pictograms and Story Grammar

# Pictograms and Story Grammar

Pictogram's aid story recall and language comprehension by providing a visual structural support for children who struggle to read or write stories. Students draw simple stick figures to represent a story narrative. Pictograms are a viable alternative for children who cannot write quickly or well due to reading/language difficulty, or are too young to write.

Pictography is the process of drawing simple pictures to represent text. Pictography is highly useful because it can convey ideas and events of a narrative without needing to resort to written language and can improve children's reading comprehension skill.

Pictography represents events in a story using simple stick like figures. Children are encouraged to draw simple stick figures that represent actions from a story grammar. Most young children can draw simple stick figures without too much difficulty. The images are produced in chronological order, and, like text, begin from the *left* of the page and move across to the *right* of the page. The drawings are able to provide a detailed representation of the events in a story with only a small handful of images.

Pictograms also provide memory and organizational support for narratives which students may struggle to verbally recount. The pictograms in this section are based on the *Guff's Journey* story.

# Pictograms for the Guff's Journey

The events depicted are events detailed in the Guff's Journey story. Guff's Journey has story grammar elements with initiating event, plan, attempts, consequences and reactions which can easily be explored using pictogram stick figures.

# Pictograms and Story Grammar Example

The clinician writes the pictograms in sequence starting with the mammoth hunt and includes all the major sequences and events in the story, finishing with Guff being found by his father. Note that the clinician adds arrows after each sequence.

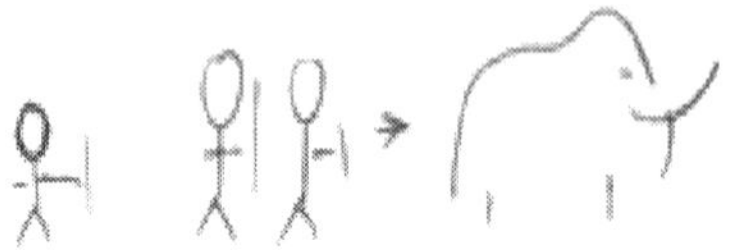

Clinician: 'At the start of the story Guff gets separated from his tribe while on a mammoth hunt.'

Clinician: 'Guff is chased by a mammoth and runs for his life.'

Clinician: 'Guff escapes the mammoth by falling down a cliff.'

Clinician: 'Guff wakes later that day laying in a ditch.'

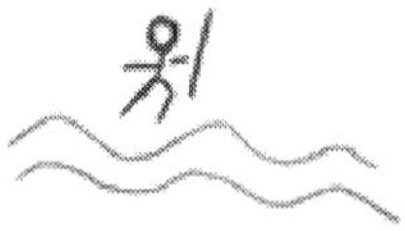

Clinician: 'Guff spends the night in the ditch and sets off the next day following a river to find his tribe.'

Clinician: 'After a day of walking Guff finds a lake and decides to rest.'

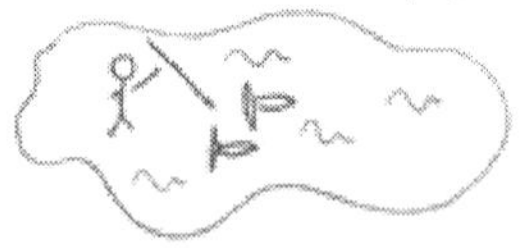

Clinician: 'Guff is hungry so he makes a spear to catch fish.'

Clinician: 'Guff cooks his catch over a fire he makes.'

Clinician: 'The smell of the cooked fish attracts a saber-toothed cat.'

Clinician: 'Guff distracts the cat and races for a nearby tree.'

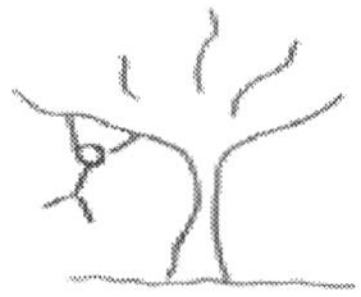

Clinician: 'Guff climbs the tree before the big cat can catch him.'

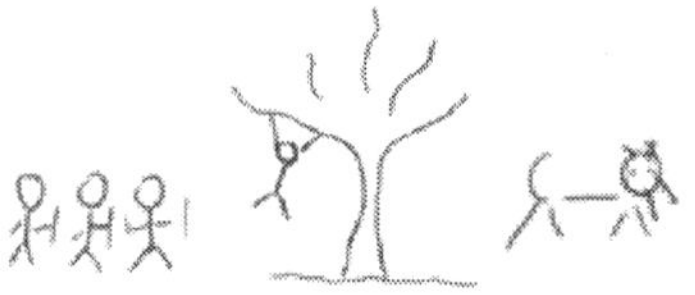

Clinician: 'Members of Guff's tribe see smoke from the fire and rescue Guff. Guff is safe.'

As can be seen from the above pictogram example, the drawings do not require any artistic skill and can be drawn very quickly. After the clinician has drafted the pictographic representation of the story events, the clinician discusses the story with the student.

The events in the pictogram can be coded as *setting, complication*, *attempts*, *internal response* and *resolution*. The clinician then discusses the events with the student.

**Clinician**: 'The story is set in the prehistoric world and Guff chooses to go along the mountain pass. This is our setting for the story. The story begins with Guff separated from his tribe following a mammoth hunt gone wrong and needing to find his way home to his family and tribe. This is the first part of the story and is what we call the initiating event. It's called the *initiating event* because it's the beginning of the story and what sets the story in motion. Guff is concerned and frightened about being separated from his tribe but he is resourceful, clever and very brave. We call this Guff's *internal response and* it is how he feels about his situation of being cut off from his tribe but determined to find his way home and the decision he needs to make to find his way home. Guff's plan is simple: he needs to find his way home. He chooses to follow a river because it may lead him to his family. Guff makes many *attempts* and endures *complications* on his journey down the river and eventually finds a lake, catches a fish and makes a fire. A saber-toothed cat is attracted by the smell of the cooked fish. Guff takes the only option open to him and climbs a nearby tree. The *resolution* is Guff escapes the big cat and his tribe and father find him safe up the tree. Guff is relieved and happy to have survived the dangers of the prehistoric world alone.'

## Recommended Pictogram Story Grammar Sequence

- Read the *Guff's Journey* story and then use the story itself to create pictograms that sequence the events in the story.
- After students have read the *Guff's Journey* story, encourage them to talk about the events in the story. Students are to provide an oral retell of the events in the story.
- Demonstrate the sequence of events in the story modelling a story grammar using the pictograms featured in this chapter.
- Students are then to create their own pictogram using the stick figures in this section as a guide, but are encouraged to create their own figures. Remember to draw arrows to represent the flow of time and to connect of events from the story.
- Students then narrate the story using their pictograms to aid their recollection of the events from the story.

# Completed Story Map *Example*

**Story Title**

*Guff's Journey*

**Setting**: Where is the story set?

*Prehistoric Europe with lots of mountains and looks to be a cold environment.*

**Story Start**: What problem sets the story in motion?

*Guff on his first hunt becomes separated from his tribe.*

**Internal response**: What does the character feel?

*Frightened but determined to find his tribe.*

**Plan**: What does the character plan to do?

*Survive and find his way back to his family and tribe.*

**Attempts**: What does the character do about the problem?

1. *Guff initially escapes from the pursuing mammoth.*
2. *Guff then charts his way down a river, catches a fish and makes fire.*
3. *Guff escapes up a tree to escape a sabre-toothed cat.*

**Resolution**: What happens at the end? How does the character feel at the end of the story?

*Guff survives the dangers of the prehistoric world and we can infer that he feels proud to have survived alone separated from his tribe.*

# References

Collins Essential Dictionary and Thesaurus (2007) *Harper Collins Publishers*

DeKemel, K.P. (2003) Intervention in Language Arts: A Practical Guide for Speech-Language Pathologists. *Butterworth-Heinemann.*

Dorn, L.D. & Soffos, C. (2005) Teaching for Deep Comprehension *Stenhouse Publishers Portland, Maine*

Kaderavek, J & Justice, L.M. (2002) Shared Storybook Reading as an Intervention Context: Practices and Potential Pitfalls. *American Journal of Speech-Language Pathology, Vol 11. 395-406.*

Norris, J.A. (1991) From Frog to Prince: Using Written Language as a Context for Language Learning, *Topics in Language Disorders. Vol 12, 66-81*

Ukrainetz, T. (2006) Contextualized Language Intervention: Scaffolding Prek-12 Literacy Achievement *Pro-ed*

Wagner, R.K. Muse, A.E. & Tannenbaum, K.R. (2007) Vocabulary Acquisition: Implications for Reading Comprehension. *The Guilford Press*

Wallach, G.P. (2008) Language Intervention for School-Age Students: Setting Goals for Academic Success. *Mosby Elsevier*

# Appendix A

## Answer Section

# Answer Section

## Background Information

1. Neanderthals lived in what is now modern day Europe.
2. Neanderthals had bigger brains and tougher bodies.
3. Neanderthals were always on the move. They were hunter-gatherers and needed to follow herds of animals for food.
4 Neanderthals used axes and spears and flint to make fire.
5. Neanderthals created clothes from animal hide and pelts.
6. Neanderthals were excellent hunters.
7. Mammoths are similar to elephants.
8. Mammoths were covered in thick hair.
9. Saber-toothed cats are famous for having very large teeth.
10. Saber-toothed cats were broad and thickset.

## Inference Questions

1. Mammoths lived in cold environments so needed the hair to stay warm.
2. No. Most tribes were hunter-gatherers and did not build towns or villages.
3. Neanderthals were able to make fire so we can assume they cooked their food.
4. Neanderthals used sign and verbal language but not written language.
5. It is likely that Neanderthals were frightened of such fierce animals like the saber-toothed cat.
6. Mostly for hunting, thou axes could also be used to create clothes and shelter.
7. Yes. Neanderthals had a complex form of sign and verbal language.
8. Yes, likely. Neanderthals were tougher and more able to cope with a difficult environment.

## Recall of Story Details

*Story Details – Scene 1*

1. Utha was a short spear's throw from where Guff lay.
2. Dry grass.
3. Long dry grass.
4. The mammoth's breath rippled Guff's hair.
5. The mammoth suddenly stomped to where Guff lay.
6. The mammoth's tusks were curved and lethal.
7. Utha lay next to Guff's uncle Grok.

*Moments in Time – Scene 1*

1. Utha smiled at Guff first.
2. Guff describes being as a quiet as a field mouse first.
3. The mammoth approached the grass *after* Utha smiled at Guff.
4. The shaggy mane filled Guff's nostrils first.
5. The mammoth's breath rippled Guff's hair before it tore out chunks of grass.

*Making Inferences from the Story – Scene 1*

1. Utha smiled to help relax Guff and was afraid for him.
2. Any sound may have given away the tribe's hiding spot.
3. The mammoth's breath rippled Guff's hair so it must have been just above Guff.
4. The mammoth was a huge and terrifying animal so Guff was afraid.
5. Guff was sweating from nervousness and fear.

*Story Details – Scene 2*

1. Utha was trying to locate and help Guff.
2. Guff could not remember getting to his feet.
3. Guff soared through the air after being hit in the side.
4. The air was ripped from his chest.
5. Guff failed to see that the ground had stopped and that he was at the edge of a cliff.
6. Guff's legs cramped.
7. Guff was in a ditch at the bottom of a deep ravine.

*Moments in Time – Scene 2*

1. Spears soaring and buzzing happened first.
2. Guff had the air ripped from his chest before he heard his father calling to him.
3. Guff fell down the hill *after* he realized his father and uncle were scattered.
4. Guff poked his head above the ditch first.
5. Guff lay in a deep feint then his head slowly cleared.

*Making Inferences from the Story – Scene 2*

1. The mammoth or the mammoth's trunk.
2. Either shock or fear prevented him from forming words.
3. Guff was running for his life and was perhaps tunnel-visioned at that moment.
4. Guff needed his blade to survive and we can infer that Utha may have reinforced this to Guff
5. Guff was alone and in a dangerous environment.

*Story Details – Scene 3*

1. Guff had to first survive the night.
2. A fire.
3. His ancestors.
4. Guff listened for the sounds of predators.
5. Guff's head was buried in his cloak.
6. The water was cold, intense and delicious.
7. When lost, a river could lead you home.

*Moments in Time – Scene 3*

1. Guff drank the water first and then remembered his father's words.
2. Guff wrapped himself in furs first and then listened for sounds of dangerous beasts.
3. Short gusts of mist escaped form Guff's mouth first.
4. Guff drank the water after leaving the ditch.
5. Gulf gripped his spear after walking to the river.

*Making Inferences from the Story – Scene 3*

1. Guff may have felt fear but some anticipation as well.
2. Many different reasons. The sun warmed Guff's face, the sun allowed him to see his surroundings etc.
3. Guff was perhaps seeking some guidance from a higher power.
4. Guff had ice in his hair that morning.
5. The monster with long blades was a saber-toothed cat.
6. Guff needed to be able to escape any predators who chanced upon him.

*Story Details – Scene 4*

1. Guff watched for beasts that may be a threat.
2. Mountains and valleys stretched to a vast distance.
3. Guff was at the shore of a large lake.
4. The lake was like a large, flat green stone.
5. A ravine.
6. The bones of an elk.
7. He lay his upon a flat stone and closed his eyes.

*Moments in Time – Scene 4*

1. Guff watched for animals first.
2. Guff's leg throbbed first and he lay down to rest later.
3. Guff climbed the cliff first.
4. Guff found the lake first and the elk bones later.
5. Guff saw the mountains reflected in the water before he saw the elk bones.

*Making Inferences for the Story – Scene 4*

1. The scene that confronted Guff was enormous which made him feel very small.
2. Yes, a little. If there was no river further down he would have to change his plan.
3. Probably noon or the middle of the day.
4. The lake was probably very beautiful and a welcome sight after a long day of walking.
5. Guff was always looking for dangerous animals so he would have been uneasy at all times.

*Story Details – Scene 5*

1. Tiny splashes.
2. Tiny fish in the lake.
3. A spear to catch fish.
4. A three pronged spear.
5. Guff hauled the fish into the air and flicked the spear so that the fish landed on big stones.
6. To make a fire to cook the fish.
7. The sun was low in the sky suggesting late afternoon, early evening.

*Moments in Time – Scene 5*

1. The fish woke Guff who later made a spear to catch the fish.
2. Guff bound the elk bones before stepping into the water.
3. Guff caught the fish then decided to make a fire.

4. Guff made the spear first, then caught the fish then cleaned it.
5. Guff's stomach grumbled after he heard the fish splash.

*Making Inferences from the Story – Scene 5*

1. Guff was very hungry.
2. The water was freezing.
3. He was exhausted and very sore from injuries sustained the day before.
4. Yes, the sun was low in the sky indicating late afternoon, early evening.
5. Guff had seen his father make one.

*Story Details – Scene 6*

1. Leaves and bark.
2. His dark stone, which was a piece of flint for lighting fires.
3. Sparks.
4. Smoke.
5. Tufts of dried grass.
6. Delicious, slightly charred on the outside.
7. Guff threw two large branches on the fire.

*Moments in Time – Scene 6*

1. Guff gathered the bark and leaves first.
2. Guff layered strips of bark and leaves and then skewered the fish.
3. Guff blew on the small flame to make it larger then later threw on two branches.
4. Guff roasted the fish and then unwrapped the blackened leaves.
5. Guff struck the flat rock with his dark stone first, he later roasted the fish.

*Making Inferences from the Story – Scene 6*

1. The sparks could cause a fire.
2. The tiny fire may have quickly gone out.
3. The fire most probably would have gone out.
4. The leaves would protect the fish from the flames.
5. The fire provided comfort and warmth and allowed Guff to cook the fish.

*Story Details – Scene 7*

1. A saber-tooth cat.
2. Guff felt the blood drain from his face.
3. Terrible long teeth.
4. Searching for Guff's scent.
5. Guff realized to his dismay that his spear was only useful for stabbing fish.
6. To climb the tree quickly.
7. Look up at him with its yellow eyes.

*Moments in Time – Scene 7*

1. Guff climbed the tree after he threw the spear.
2. The cat sniffed the air first and then launched after Guff.
4. Guff prepared his spear before throwing it at the big cat.

5. Guff prayed to his ancestors before he threw his spear.

*Making Inference from the Story – Scene 7*

1. Blood draining from Guff's face means that he felt shock and fear.
2. We can infer that the cat was much faster than Guff and would have caught him.
3. He may not have had time to reach the tree before the cat caught him.
4. Because Guff had been found by people he knew and loved.
5. Because Guff was eager to get back to his father and safety.

## Syntax and Grammar

### Task A – Present Tense - Regular Past Tense Verbs

1. pressed
2. grazed
3. loomed
4. rippled
5. filled
6. trembled, gripped
7. thumped
8. soared, buzzed
9. tried, failed
10. sensed
11. cleared
12. shivered, huddled
13. sorted, prepared
14. snarled, bounded

### Task B – Present Tense - Irregular Past Tense Verbs

1. lay
2. ran
3. got
4. heard
5. bound
6. stood
7. flung
8. saw
9. threw, blew
10. caught
11. felt
12. crept
13. rose

### Task C: Choose the right word

1. bear
2. bait
3. muscles
4. meat
5. mist
6. night
7. pain
8. piece
9. poured
10. prey
11. rain
12. hare
13. reeds
14. rowed
15. sowed
16. weather
17. rough
18. grown
19. hauled
20. great
21. heart
22. flower
23. new
24. flee
25. flew
26. weather
27. beat
28. herd

Task D – Syntax Exercises – Compound Sentences

1. The water was cold **and** the air was crisp.
2. Guff walked quickly **but** he didn't get far.
3. The fish ate the bait **so** Asa caught the fish.
4. Guff could take his axe **or** *he* could take his spear.
5. Asa fished all day **yet** *she* didn't catch a fish.
6. Utha chased the deer **but** *he* couldn't get close.
7. The forest was dark **and** the ground was wet.
8. Asa could go fishing **or** hunting.
9. The cliff was steep **but** Guff felt confident.
10. Guff's boots were torn **and** his spear was broken.

12. The day was cloudy **but** hot.
13. Asa carried her fishing rod **and** basket.
14. Guff climbed the tree **yet** *he* could not reach the nest.
15. Asa cleaned the fish **so** *she* could eat *it*.
16. Guff took aim **and** threw his spear.
17. Guff couldn't get warm **so** *he* made a fire.
18. Guff climbed a tree **so** *he* could steal bird eggs.
19. Asa walked to the river **and** filled *her* jug with water.

### Task E: Syntax Exercises – Contracting Compound Sentences

1. Guff caught the fish. Asa cleaned the fish.
2. Asa helped her mother to cook. Asa helped her father to make a fire.
3. Guff climbed the mountain. Guff looked out over the ocean.
4. The eagle swooped down. The eagle narrowly missed Guff's head.
5. Guff wanted to walk. Asa wanted to run.
6. Utha scaled and cleaned the fish. His family could eat the fish.
7. Asa was tired. Asa climbed to the top of the mountain.
8. Guff heard the cat growling. Guff spun around quickly.
9. Utha repaired his axe. Guff sharpened his spear.

### Task F: Syntax Exercises – Creating Complex Sentences

1. Guff ate the fish because he was hungry.
2. Asa wore her bearskin rug because it was cold.
3. Utha, who is very brave, is a great hunter.
4. After Guff made the fire, he cooked the fish.
5. Guff put the shell into his pouch, which was full of trinkets.
6. Before Utha went hunting, he sharpened his spear.
7. Asa hid from the cat that hunted her.
8. The mammoth charged Guff who ran for his life.
9. Asa cooked the raw fish until it was ready to eat.
10. Guff touched his dark stone, which hung around his neck.

### Task G: Syntax Exercises – Contracting Complex Sentences

1. Guff did not cross the river. The river was too deep.
2. Asa was very quiet. Asa was hunting rabbits.
3. Guff was on the open plain. Guff was in danger.
4. Utha hunted for mammoth. Utha checked his spear for cracks.
5. Guff scaled the cliff face. Guff's arms became tired.
6. It was hot. Guff loved to swim in the river.
7. It was very dangerous to approach a mammoth. The entire was there as a support.
8. Utha, the tribal elder, was very brave. Utha led the hunting party on its first great hunt of the spring.

### Task H: Syntax Exercises – Expanding Sentences with Adjectives

1. Asa washed her hands in the clear water.
2. Utha is a cunning, strong and powerful hunter.
3. Guff walked in the dark, leafy forest.
4. The mammoth raised its massive, shaggy head.
5. Guff hunted the large mammoth herd with his tribe.
6. Utha collected sweet, sticky honey from the beehive.
7. The old tree's branches rose high above the tall forest.
8. The strong wind blew through Asa's hair.
9. Utha ran his life as the ferocious saber-toothed cat attacked.

### Task H: Syntax Exercises – Arrangement of Words

1. The tribe walked up the hill.
2. The mammoth roared loudly.
3. Guff woke the next morning.
4. The mammoths ate the long grass.
5. Guff his behind the bush.
6. Guff decided to follow the river.
7. Guff rested under an old tree.
8. Guff waded into the cold water.
9. Guff walked along the river's edge.
10. Guff was in terrible danger.
11. Guff wrapped the fish in leaves.
12. Guff roasted the fish over the fire.
13. Guff ran for his life to the tree.

### Task J: Syntax Exercises – Assembling Paragraphs

1. Guff came to a steep cliff. Guff gripped the hard rock with his fingers. He carefully climbed down the cliff-face. Guff slipped but held onto the rock. Finally, with a gentle hop, Guff landed at the bottom.

2 Asa felt the storm coming before she saw it. The rain came down in sheets of water. The lightening terrified Asa and the thunder sounded like huge drums. Asa hid in the shelter.

3. The saber-toothed cat approached Guff, snarling. Guff thrust his spear at the cat and backed away slowly. When the big cat pounced, Guff ran for his life and climbed the tree just in time.
4. The river was deep and swift but Guff needed to cross it. Guff stepped into the water and felt it surge past his legs. He slipped and fell into the flowing water. Guff was strong and able to swim across the mighty river. Coughing up water, Guff made it to the opposite riverbank.

## Critical Thinking *(Problem Solving)*

### Task A: Critical Thinking Exercises

1. rope, strong boots
2. rope knife

3. fishing line, bait
4. dry wood, flint
5. pot, campfire
6. spear, blade
7. woolen cloak, woolen hat
8. bait, net
9. mud bricks, straw
10. shelter, roof
11. flat dry stone, blade
12. knife, string/twine

## Task B:The Missing Piece

2. Guff pulls himself up the tree after grasping the branch with his left hand.
3. Utha carefully and quietly approaches the deer without it noticing his presence.
4. Guff runs to a nearby tree to escape the saber-toothed cat's claws.
5. Utha attaches a water-tight roof to the shelter.
6. In the nest were bird eggs which Guff took from the nest.
7. Asa builds the small flame into a fire and colas that are best for cooking.
8. The bull mammoth attacks the hunters and scatters the hunters.
9. The branches are pruned and cleaned and assembled to be tied together with twine.

## Task C: Which is easier for the character to do?

1. **Possible response** – Ride a mammoth, mainly because fighting a saber-tooth cat with your bare hands seems vaguely suicidal.
2. **Possible response** - Light a fire with flint, although if the wood was wet it might actually take longer to cut down a tree with an axe than it would to make wet wood burn.
3. **Possible response** – Swim across a river that is swiftly flowing. Though if the water was *surging and/or really cold,* you would sooner climb a tall mountain than dip a toe in *that* water.
4. **Possible response** – Spearing a fish, depending on skill level. Swimming across a swiftly flowing river is never a good idea.
5. **Possible response** – Eagle's nest, hunting a mammoth herd alone is never going to end well.
6. **Possible response** - Fish with fishing line seems to be a lot easier than spearing a fish, though spearing a fish may be quicker depending on skill level.
7. **Possible response** – A knife, because it's a much finer instrument than an axe.

## Task D: What is the problem?

1. Guff could possibly get frostbite. At the very least, he will have very cold feet.
2. A broken spear against a saber-toothed cat means that Utha has no weapon.
3. Guff could become very cold or could even develop hypothermia, or get struck by lightning.
4. Asa may have to make her way in the dark and potentially become lost.
5. Utha would have no chance to defend himself against two such lethal predators.

6. Guff will not have the tools to make fire which means in winter he could not keep warm.
7. The nuts and fruits may fall from her bag.
8. Guff could become lost very quickly if he doesn't know which direction he is facing.
9. The shelter will potentially not be constructed well.
10. The tribe may not find enough to eat and could starve in the unforgiving winter.

## Task E: How to avoid the problem.

2. Asa should have stayed within sight of the camp or marked trees and rocks to find her way back to camp easily.
3. Guff should have tied the spear tightly or alerted his father.
4. Utha should have been aware of the lack of twine and made some new twine.
5. Guff should have ensured that the pouch was safe and secure before gathering food.
6. Utha should have done a better job and made sure that the roof was secure.
7. Guff probably should have mountain climbed on a clearer day if he wished to see the view.
8. Utha should either have not left the shelter or carried a weapon of some type.
9. Asa should have carried her basket with her.

## Task F: Problem solving tough situations

1a. Guff and Asa have been separated from their tribe and are in a tricky spot.

1b. Mammoths are wild animals and very large and dangerous.

1c. Their best option may be to wait until the mammoth herd have moved on.

2a. Guff is exposed on a cliff face and cannot go up or down without difficulty.

2b. Guff hugs the cliff face fiercely because he is frightened of being knocked off it by the large eagle.

2c. Guff may be wise to abandon the climb and return to the ground.

3a. Utha is alone and unlikely to win against a mammoth.

3b. The hunting party panicked and Utha stayed because he is very brave and very confident.

3c. Utha could run or he could throw the spear at the mammoth.

4a. This is a huge problem for Guff because he is alone and has to fend off two fierce predators.

4b. Guff has no chance to run around the saber-toothed cats because they are too fast.

4c. Guff could attempt to climb down the cliff face just out of reach of the saber-toothed cats and hang on to rocks until the cats lose interest and leave.

5a. This is a problem because Guff and Asa have spent half the day gathering food, so essentially have wasted the day.

5b. Guff and Asa perhaps should not have gone swimming until they had returned the food to the camp. Also, Guff and Asa should have made certain that the food was hidden or out of reach of forest animals before they went for a swim.

5c. Guff and Asa can spend the remainder of the day foraging for food once mor

# Inference

## Task A: Inference – Level 1

1. We can infer that Guff had been fishing because he packed away fishing line and fish, which he had probably caught that day.
2. We can infer that Asa's fire making equipment had become soaked by the rain making it difficult to use.
3. Guff had difficulty keeping up because he had an injured ankle, which caused him pain.
4. The weather was stormy and very cold.
5. We can infer that snow had fallen throughout the night.
6. The day may have started cold, but had warmed up sufficiently for Guff to remove the heavy furs from his body.
7. We can infer that Utha had been making a spear of some kind.
8. We can infer that Guff is at the top of a hill or mountain.
9. We can infer that it is dawn or very early in the morning.
10. The light and heat source is the sun.
11. We can infer that Guff is seated at a riverbank and that he is fishing.
12. Asa was cleaning and cooking fish.

### Task A: Inference – Level 2

1a. A mammoth herd up close would be quite intimidating and frightening.
1b. The tribe approached with stealth because they needed to get close to the herd and any noise may have scattered the herd.
1c. We can infer that food will be scarce in winter.
1d. The ground was possibly covered in ice which made the ground '*scrunchy.*'
2a. Asa had been running very fast to get home quickly which caused her to run out of breath.
2b. The tanning hides may have been damaged by the falling rain.
2c. Asa knew that she had to get back to the camp quickly to help her mother.
2d. We can infer that the ball of flashing light was lightning.
3a. Guff was standing very still so as not to alert the fish to his presence.
3b. The swift, dark forms were fish.
3c. Guff had been standing in cold water, which caused his teeth to chatter.
3d. The silver creature was a fish.
4a. Utha was using tools to make a fire.
4b. Utha had used the hardwood often because it was stained from frequent use.
4c. Thin dry grass will catch fire easily.
4d. Utha blew gently to ensure that the tiny flame did not flicker out.
5a. The birds were startled by the approach of the saber-toothed cat.
5b. The saber-toothed cat.
5c. Utha was very fit and strong and his arms were tensed in anticipation.
5d. The great feline was a saber-tooth cat. *Feline* indicates a cat of some kind.

# Appendix B

## Reading Error, Reading Comprehension and Narrative Analysis Forms

# Reading Error Record Form

Student: ____________________ Date: ________ Total Words: _________

Reading Time: _______ Reading Rate: ________ (*words per min*). To tally words per minute, count the time it took the student to complete the passage. Then divide the total no. of words in passage by total time (*in seconds*). Reading Rate = no. of words / time x 60.

## Reading Errors *(Accuracy Errors)*

Words Replaced ________ Words Deleted ________

Words Added ________ Words Incorrect ________

Accuracy Errors ________

## Reading Errors *(Fluency Errors)*

Words Repeated ________ Pauses While Reading ________

Word by Word ________

Self Correction ________

Fluency Errors ________

Add the total number of **accuracy** errors and **fluency** errors.

Combined Errors (ac + fl) _______

Divide **accuracy errors** and **fluency errors** by **combined errors** and multiply by 100 to work out the percentage of errors in a passage.

Like this...

*Accuracy Errors*

No. of **accuracy errors** ____ /_____ **combined errors** = _____ x 100 = _____ % **ac**

*Fluency Errors*

No. of **fluency errors** ____ /_____ **combined errors** = _____ x 100 = _____ % **fl**

# Question Comprehension Analysis – Factual Questions Form

| | | |
|---|---|---|
| Student: | Date: | Year Level: |
| School: | Book Title: | |

## Factual Questions

Score each question 0, 1, or 2.

Question 1:

Students Response:

Score:

Question 2:

Students Response:

Score:

Question 3:

Students Response:

Score:

### Factual Question Score Guide

| | |
|---|---|
| **0** | Inaccurate and incomplete |
| **1** | Partially correct, logical but not complete |

# Question Comprehension Analysis – Surface Level Inference Form

| | | |
|---|---|---|
| Student: | Date: | Year Level: |
| School: | Book Title: | |

## Surface Inference Questions

Score each question 0, 1, or 2.

Question 1:

Students Response:

Score:

Question 2:

Students Response:

Score:

Question 3:

Students Response:

Score:

| Surface Level Inference Question Score Guide | |
|---|---|
| **0** | Inaccurate and incomplete |
| **1** | Partially correct, logical but not complete |

# Question Comprehension Analysis – Deep Level Inference Form

Student: Date: Year Level:

School: Book Title:

## Deep Level Inference Questions

Score each question 0, 1, or 2.

Question 1:

Students Response:

Score:

Question 2:

Students Response:

Score:

Question 3:

Students Response:

Score:

| Deep Level Inference Question Score Guide | |
|---|---|
| **0** | Inaccurate and incomplete |
| **1** | Partially correct, logical but not complete |

# Oral Retell *Guff's Journey* - Transcription

Student: ________________ DOB: _______ Examiner: ________________

School: _________________ Date: ___________

Record the student's oral retell of the story. Most modern cell or mobile phones have a voice recording app as standard, which can record a student's oral retell. Transcribe the student's retell onto the space provided.

Instructions: '*Let's look at this story together. It's a story set in prehistoric times about a boy named Guff. You need to listen carefully while I tell the story. When I've finished it will then be your turn to tell the story. Tell me everything you can about the story and make it the best you can.*'

____________________________________________________________

____________________________________________________________

____________________________________________________________

____________________________________________________________

____________________________________________________________

____________________________________________________________

____________________________________________________________

____________________________________________________________

____________________________________________________________

____________________________________________________________

____________________________________________________________

____________________________________________________________

# Oral Retell – Macrostructure Analysis

| Story Element | Present | Absent |
|---|---|---|
| Beginning<br>(One day, Once upon a time…) | | |
| Character Introduction<br>Guff and his father Utha | | |
| Initiating Event<br>(Guff is on his first hunt…) | | |
| Plan: Cognitive verb used…<br>(Guff knew he needed to be quiet….) | | |
| 1. Attempt to solve the problem<br>(Guff ran for his life to escape the mammoth) | | |
| Obstacle<br>(Guff fall down a hill and lands in a ditch…) | | |
| 2. Attempt to solve the problem<br>(Guff follows a river to find his tribe and home…) | | |
| Consequence<br>(Guff makes a fire to cook a fish and attracts a saber tooth cat) | | |
| Reaction/Resolution<br>(Guff races to a tree and climbs up to escape the saber-tooth cat) | | |
| Closing Event<br>(The fire has been seen by Guff's tribe who rescue Guff from the big cat.) | | |

Indicate the level of prompts needed for the student to complete the oral retell. Please tick the appropriate box that best represented the use of prompts.

- ☐ None: The student completed the oral retell effectively without prompts.
- ☐ General prompts: The student needed some prompts, *'you're doing well…'*
- ☐ Specific prompts: *'Tell me how the story begins …how did he feel?*

# Oral Retell – Macrostructure Analysis

| Story Element | Present | Absent |
|---|---|---|
| Beginning | | |
| Character Introduction | | |
| Initiating Event | | |
| Plan: Cognitive verb used… | | |
| 1. Attempt to solve the problem | | |
| Obstacle | | |
| 2. Attempt to solve the problem | | |
| Consequence | | |
| Reaction/Resolution | | |
| Closing Event | | |

Indicate the level of prompts needed for the student to complete the oral retell. Please tick the appropriate box that best represented the use of prompts.

- ☐ **None**: The student completed the oral retell effectively without prompts.
- ☐ **General prompts**: The student needed some prompts, *'you're doing well…'*
- ☐ **Specific prompts**: *'Tell me how the story begins …how did he feel?*

# Appendix C

## Intervention Graphic Organizers

# Pre-story Background Map

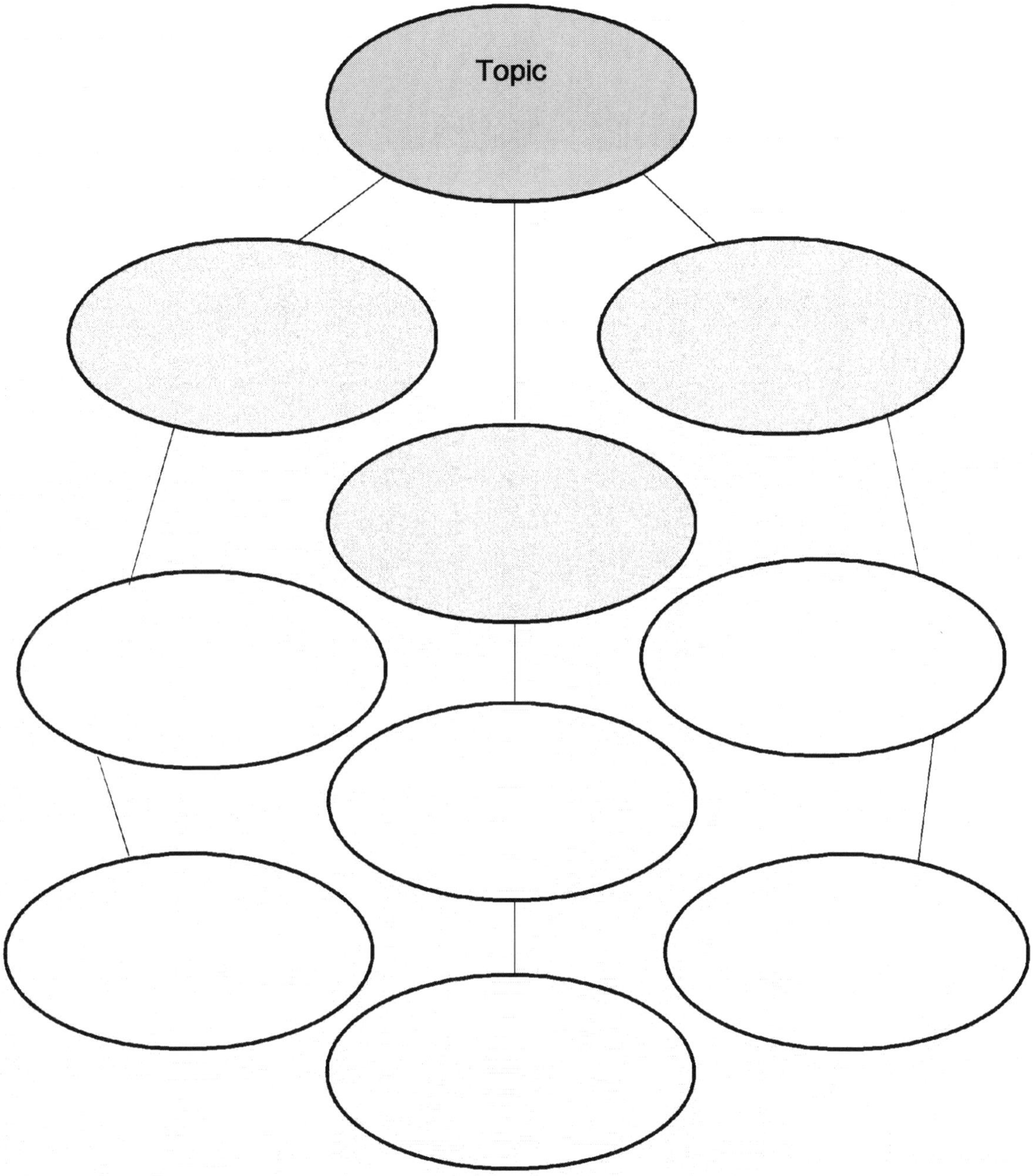

# Vocabulary Map

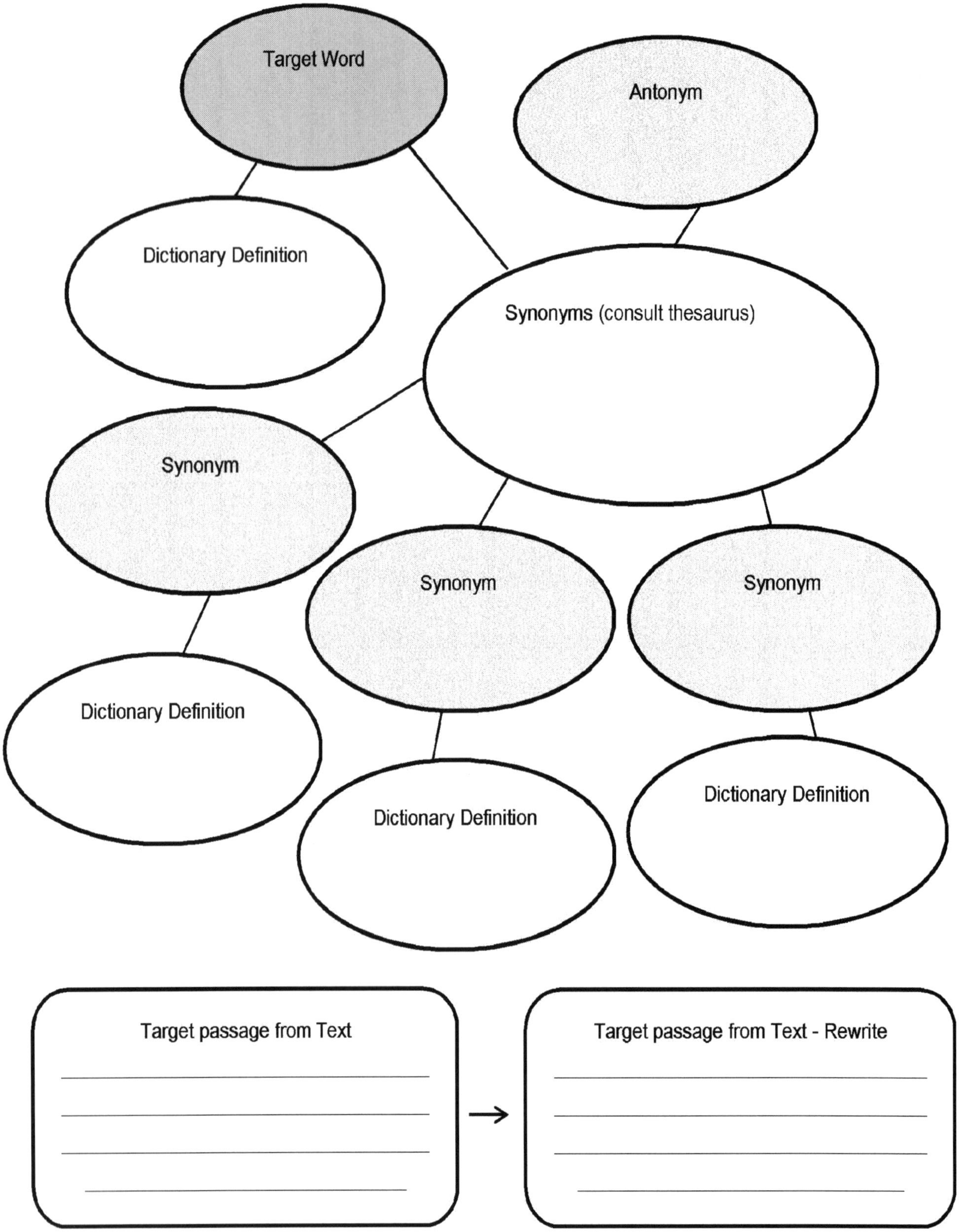
Target Word
Antonym
Dictionary Definition
Synonyms (consult thesaurus)
Synonym
Synonym
Synonym
Dictionary Definition
Dictionary Definition
Dictionary Definition
Target passage from Text
Target passage from Text - Rewrite

# Semantic Map for Nouns

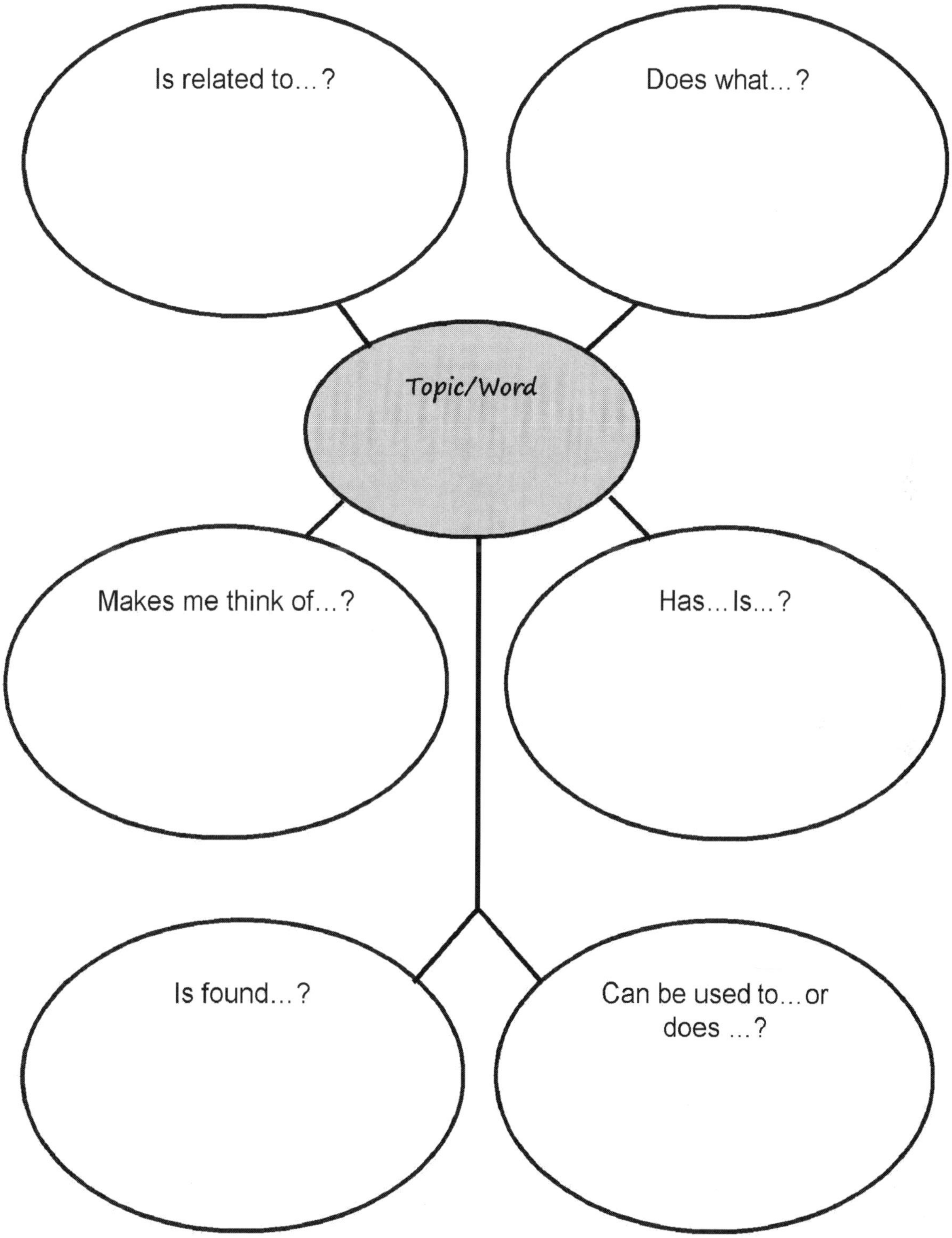

# Semantic Map for Adjectives

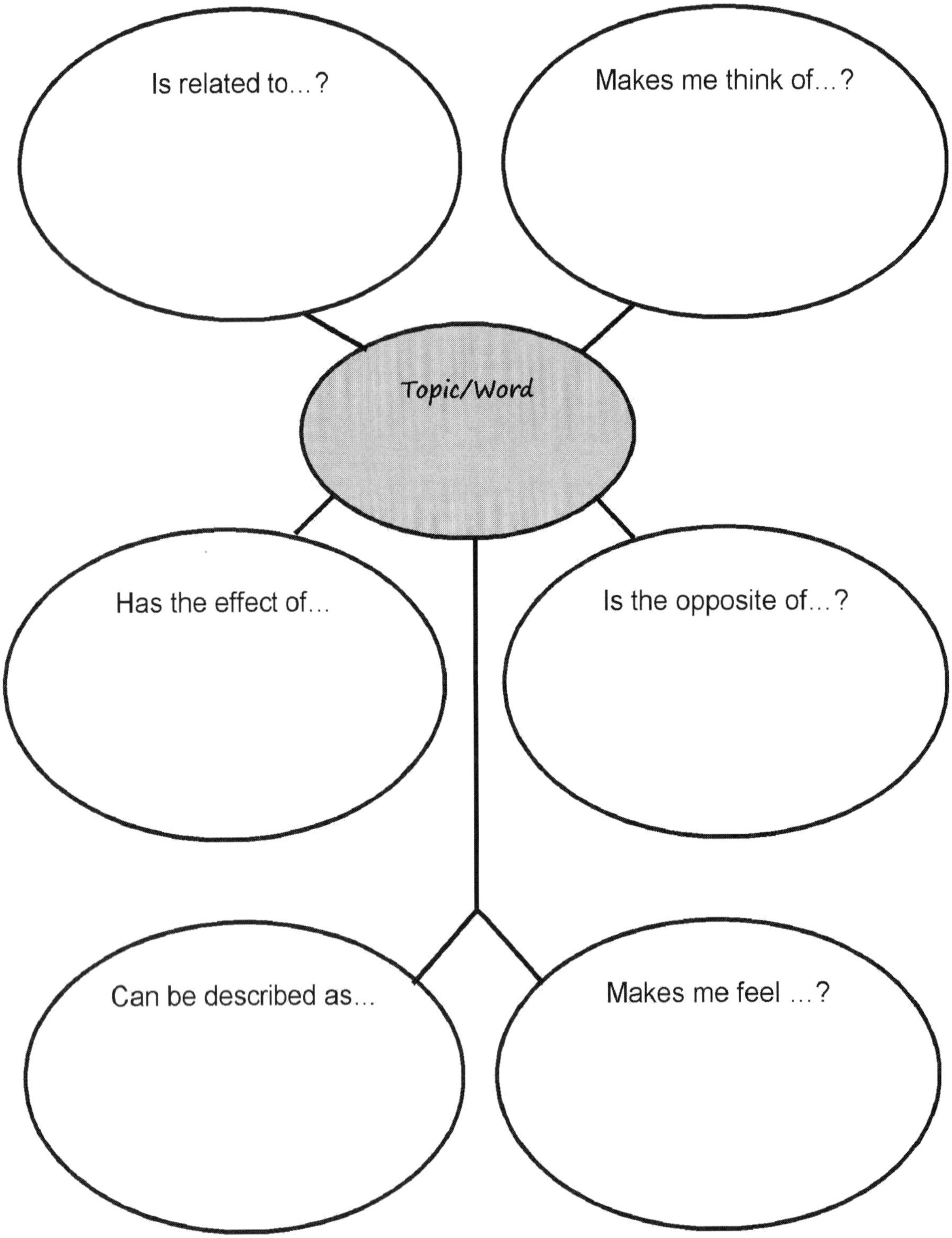

# Story Map

**Story Title**

Setting: Where is the story set?

Story Start: What problem sets the story in motion?

Internal response: What does the character feel?

Plan: What does the character plan to do?

Attempts: What does the character do about the problem?

1

2

3

4

5

Resolution: What happens at the end? How does the character feel at the end of the story?

# Character Map

Character's name

Age and Gender

Character Traits

Character's Lifestyle

Where the Character Lives

Description of the Character

# Dictionary Alphabet Guide

a b c d e

f g h i j k

l m n o p

q r s t u v

w x y z

Remember to use the **guide words** at the top of the dictionary. The guide words help you to locate your target word. The guide word at the top of the left side of the page repeats the *first* word; the guide word at the top right-hand page repeats the *last* word on that page. If you use the alphabet guide correctly, your target word should be somewhere on the double page spread, between the first and last guide words.

## How to use this guide

- To find the word you are looking for you without wasting time and effort you need to have an intimate knowledge of how the alphabet is arranged.
- This guide provides a visual model of the alphabet, which helps to speed up the process of looking for new words in a dictionary.
- For example let's say you want to find the word **goal**. First letter is **g**, we turn to the first page in the **g** section. All words on the first page start with **ga**. If we scan down the **alphabet guide** we locate the letter **o**, which is some distance from the letter **a** on the alphabet guide. This allows us to scan the **g** section till we get to **go**.
- It should be then an easy task to find **goa**. The first word in this section is **goad**. Four or five words further along we should find **goal**.

# Vocabulary Knowledge Rating Chart

The **rating chart** measures a student's understanding of a target concept. The rating system is subjective in manner but provides a convenient and relatively accurate measure of a student's competence with a newly learnt concept or word.

| Score | Description | | |
|---|---|---|---|
| Score the student's response/s, as best can be determined, in the appropriate column | 0. The student has no real understanding of the target word or concept.<br>1. The student has some understanding of the target word or concept, but has trouble describing it or writing it.<br>2. The student has good knowledge of the target word or concept and can describe it and write it well when prompted.<br>3. The student has very good understanding of the target word or concept and uses it correctly in context, written and verbal. | | |
| | Word/Concept | Word/Concept | Word/Concept |
| | ______<br>______ | ______<br>______ | ______<br>______ |
| Date ______ | Score ______ | Score ______ | Score ______ |
| Date ______ | Score ______ | Score ______ | Score ______ |
| Date ______ | Score ______ | Score ______ | Score ______ |
| Date ______ | Score ______ | Score ______ | Score ______ |
| Date ______ | Score ______ | Score ______ | Score ______ |
| Date ______ | Score ______ | Score ______ | Score ______ |
| Date ______ | Score ______ | Score ______ | Score ______ |
| Date ______ | Score ______ | Score ______ | Score ______ |

# Appendix D

## Example Comprehension Questions

# Comprehension Question Example

- Fact Based Question: A question that has a specific answer and that is clearly stated in the text. (What did the character wear?)

- Surface Level Inference Question: A question which asks about something that is implied or hinted at in the text. (Why was the character frightened?)

- Deep Level Inference Question: A question that does not rely on textual information. The reader must draw on world and word knowledge, and problem solving abilities. (Was the character angry or just playing? Would you be angry in the same situation?)

# Guff's Journey Story – Comprehension Questions

## Scene 1

### Fact Based Questions

What did Guff need to be as quiet as?

What loomed above the hunters?

What was between the tribe's spears and fat calves?

### Surface Level Inference Questions

Was the bull muloth close to Guff? How do we know this?

Why couldn't Guff breathe well?

Was Utha fit and strong? What hints at this?

### Deep Level Inference Questions

Why was it important for Guff to lay as quiet as a field mouse?

Why were the *fat calves* the target of the hunt?

What does it mean that Guff's heart flipped like a fish?

## Scene 2

### Fact Based Questions

What buzzed through the air like insects?

What happened to Guff when he struck the hard dirt?

What was Utha doing above the confusion?

### Surface Level Inference Questions

Why might Guff have had difficulty forming words at that point?

What was *shadowing* Guff as he ran?

Why did Guff fail to see that the ground had vanished from under him?

### Deep Level Inference Questions

Why are the mountains described as pitiless?

What are the last wisps of gold and what does it signify when they fade to nothing?

Why is it so significant and dangerous that Guff is alone for the first time in his life?

## Scene 3

### Fact Based Questions

What bounced in Guff's head?

What did Guff begin to do with first light?

What was in Guff's hair when dawn broke?

### Shallow Level Inference Questions

Why was Guff so fearful of making sounds at night?

What animal had teeth like long blades?

Was it cold that morning? What tells us this?

### Deep Level Inference Questions

Why did Guff have faith that he would find his father?

Why might Guff feel joy when dawn broke?

Why was the drinking of the fresh water so important to Guff, physical and mentally?

## Scene 4

### Fact Based Questions

What did Guff watch for?

What are the otters eyes described as being like?

What blocked Guff's path at one point?

### Shallow Level Inference Questions

Why did Guff feel like an ant?

Why was the appearance of the lake soothing for Guff?

Was the lake's surface choppy and rough? What tells us this?

### Deep Level Inference Questions

What do you think caused the mist to leave the valley?

At about what time was it when Guff reached the shore of the lake?

Why did Guff feel like an ant and why did that frighten him?

## Scene 5

### Fact Based Questions

What was the water described as being?

What stabbed the surface close to where Guff stood?

How big was the fish?

### Shallow Level Inference Questions

Why should Guff not stand in the water for too long?

Why was it important that Guff not move while standing in the water?

Was it early or late in the day?

### Deep Level Inference Questions

Why was it potentially dangerous to make a fire?

Why was Guff so intent on catching fish to eat?

Is Guff skilful with his hands? What tells us this?

## Scene 6

### Fact Based Questions

What did Guff wear around his neck?

What did Guff place on the flat rock?

What was the dark stone shaped like?

### Shallow Level Inference Questions

Why would Guff consider his dark stone to be more valuable than his spear or blade?

Why did Guff blow on the small twist of smoke?

Why did Guff's stomach rumble?

### Deep Level Inference Questions

Why is it important to his survival that Guff is able to make fire?

Why do you think Guff chose green leaves from the water to wrap the fish in before placing the fish in the fire?

How was Guff feeling after eating the fish and sitting by the fire? What makes you think that?

## Scene 7

### Fact Based Questions

What appeared out of the corner of Guff's eye?

What did Guff feel drain from his face?

What did Guff realize to his dismay?

### Shallow Level Inference Questions

Why was Guff dismayed to realize he only had the water spear?

Why was the creature described as *death*?

Why was the beast off balance for a moment and why did that give Guff a chance?

### Deep Level Inference Questions

Why did the tree shudder after the cat slammed into it?

What emotions would Guff be feeling when he saw his father approach?

Why did Guff's father watch Guff as he slept that night and was he there all night?

# Appendix E

## Journey Home

## Oral Narrative Board Game

As an option, **Appendix D** is available to print and download from speechlanguage-resources.com. The Language Comprehension book is perfect bound which can make photocopying a little tricky at times. So the download option is for those who don't wish to stretch the book's binding. **Appendix D** along with the other chapters in the book can be found on this web address:

https://www.speechlanguage-resources.com/journey-home-program.html

Type the above code directly into your internet browser's address bar and then click on the arrow. This → should take you direct to the **Journey Home Program** page.

Do not type the code into the search engine box, but the address bar, which is located close to the top of the browser. On the webpage, you will be able to download and print the **Appendix** activities and playing board. The playing board can be printed as either A4 or A3 size.

# Journey Home

## Oral Narrative Board Game - Introduction

The Journey Home oral narrative game and activities is an extension of the *Guff's Journey* story. In the original story, students can relate to Guff's feeling of isolation as he becomes separated from his tribe. Students are prompted to respond to Guff's bravery and resourcefulness as he struggles to survive in the dangerous prehistoric world.

The Journey Home game harnesses elements from the original *Guff's Journey* story to make a unique and exciting board game. Characters from the original story feature, such as *Guff*, the *mammoth* and the *saber-toothed cat.* The game introduces new characters such as Guff's sister *Asa*, and animals such as the *Haast eagle* and the *terror bird.* Encourage your students to search for these animals in encyclopedias that feature extinct prehistoric animals.

A natural extension of the game was to combine the events in the *Journey Home* game with story grammar principles. This can be an effective and enjoyable means of teaching story-writing and oral narrative structure to students. The strategy has the potential to be effective because students are interested in the characters' adventures while playing the game. In addition, the myriad events in the game give students loads of information with which to construct an original story. The story grammar maps help bind events together and gives shape and structure to stories.

## Three Sections

The program is composed of *three* sections. The *first* part of the program focuses on the game mechanics and the rules of the game. The *second* part of the program features the tools needed to encourage students to retell the events of the story. The *third* and final section guides students' attempts to record events of the game and ultimately write their own stories. The goal is for your students to learn and practice story retell and writing skills. The game is designed as a basis for students to learn story grammar rules; or the game can be played simply as a fun board

## Learn Within a Fun Context

Board games are a useful tool for teaching difficult language concepts. Story grammar can be a difficult concept for students to grasp. Yet if story grammar rules are learnt within an enjoyable play based context, then the concepts and processes become potentially more manageable for students. For the many students who find story writing a difficult process, then a board game, though offering similar challenges, provides a more user-friendly and engaging context in which to learn.

## Journey Home Board Game – Suggested Sequence

Part of the strength of the Journey Home game is that by simply playing the game, students get to experience what it might be like to be Guff or Asa living in a harsh wilderness. Students may feel frustration for their characters when things start to go wrong or the joy of victory when their character makes it to the village first. Students are prompted to have an emotional connection to the events in the game.

## Detail the Character's Experiences

After students have played the game, their characters' experiences can be jotted down onto paper. Students will begin to have a rough skeleton of a potential story, with a *beginning, middle* and *end*. Students can then use the story grammar worksheets to draft an *initial plan*. The **character profiles** on pages 238-242 are an excellent source for vivid words and phrases. Encourage students to use the character profiles to explore new and descriptive words, phrases and ideas to add extra colour and depth to their stories.

- Read the program and then play the Journey Home game several times to acquaint your students with the mechanics of the game. Students should learn the rules quickly but may need a guiding hand early on.
- After students have played the game, encourage them to talk about the events in the game.
- Write down, in draft form, the sequence of events in the game.

- Students are then to write down a rough draft of a story using the story grammar map as a guide.
- Students complete their stories using the character profile to assist in adding colour and variety to their stories.
- Before your students play the game for the first time, ask them to examine the playing board. Note the titles on page 224 and discuss what types of animals are pictured.
- Discuss the time period represented in the game. The game is set in prehistoric times, and the animals pictured are all extinct. Discuss the meaning of the word *extinction*.
- Reflect on the fact that the characters have three possible routes they can take to reach the village. *The Dark Forest*, the *Raging River*, and the *Mountain Pass*. Prompt your students to think about the relative dangers of each journey.
- Read through the game rules and then begin the game. Prompt students to read the instructions on each chart, dependent on reading skills.

# Journey Home Board Game

Welcome to *Journey Home*, the game that charts Guff the Neanderthal boy's long and hazardous journey home. The game is set in prehistoric times when fearsome animals such as saber-toothed cats and terror birds roamed the land. Your task is to guide your character to the safety of the village. The game has three initial separate paths: the *Dark Forest,* the *Mountain Path* and the *Raging River.* Be careful, for each path presents its own dangers. Once your character has braved the early challenges, he/she must confront the mighty mammoth and the ferocious terror bird. Only then will your character be able to reach the safety of the Neanderthal camp.

## Game Rules

- All players roll the dice. Highest number goes first. Players begin first turn in the top left corner as detailed on the map on page 225.

- Before play begins, each player must roll a dice and consult the alternate journeys chart. On a score of 1-2 the character travels down the *Raging River*, on a score of 2-3 the character journeys through the *Dark Forest*, while on a score of 5-6 the character treks over the *Mountain Pass*. The charts on pages 226-231 provides extra information for each setting.

- The *Journey Home* game has place names and starting and end points. The place names are not printed on the game board but can be quickly located by using the Board Map featured on page 225. The map also *suggests* prehistoric animal placement. The animals can either be placed at the beginning of the game or held back until a character is confronted by the animal.

Each path ultimately leads to the river crossing. To cross the river, consult the river crossing chart. Once your character crosses the river, he/she will have to confront the mighty mammoth and the fearsome terror bird before reaching the safety of the Neanderthal camp. The first to successfully navigate the dangers, escape from the predators and safely reach the Neanderthal camp wins the game.

# Journey Home Board Map

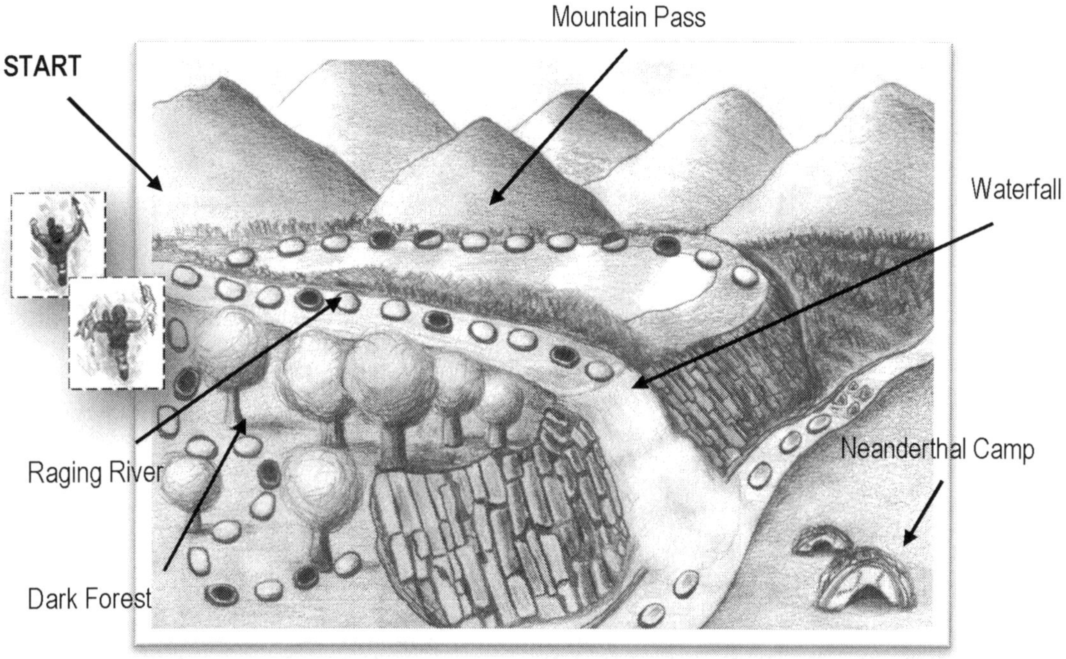


# Suggested Prehistoric Animal Placement

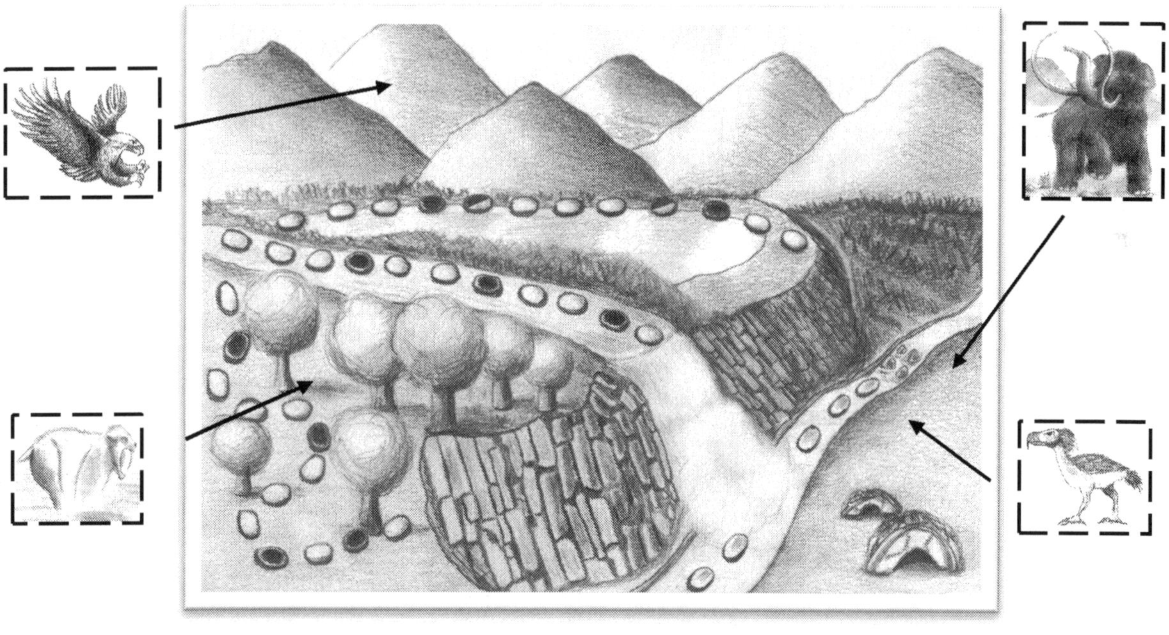

# Alternate Journey Chart

| Dice Roll | Alternate Journey Chart |
|---|---|
| 1-2 | You must navigate your way down the Raging River on a raft. Roll a dice and consult the chart before starting. |
| 3-4 | You must brave the hazards of the Dark Forest. Watch out for the saber-toothed cat! |
| 5-6 | The mountain pass is no place for a child. You must be very watchful. Don't let the Great Eagle see you! |

# The Raging River

If you roll a 1 at any point while on the river or land on a dark stone, this indicates that you have fallen off the log. *Lose a turn.*

| Dice Roll | The Raging River - Beginning |
|---|---|
| 1-2 | You attempt to jump onto a log that is flowing down the river. You miss and fall into the freezing water. *Lose a Turn* |
| 3-6 | You leap onto a log that is flowing down the river and successfully balance on the log. *Go forward 2 spaces.* |

# The Raging River

| Dice Roll | The Raging River - Waterfall |
|---|---|
| 1-2 | Your log tumbles over the waterfall. You land in the water at the bottom gasping for breath. *Lose 2 turns.* |
| 3-4 | You see the waterfall in time and guide the log to the river bank. *Lose a turn* as you climb down the cliff. |
| 5-6 | You come to the edge of the waterfall. The log tumbles over the edge, you dive into the water and surface at the bottom of the waterfall. *Next turn, continue your journey on the stone that is closest to the waterfall.* |

| Dice Roll | Dark Forest - Saber-Toothed Cat |
|---|---|
| 1-2 | With a roar the cat leaps. You evade the cat's attack and run for your life! You quickly climb a tree. *Lose a turn.* |
| 3-4 | You hear the cat approach. You run back the way you came. *Go back 3 spaces.* |
| 5-6 | The cat launches but you evade its attack. The cat loses the scent. *Go forward 1 space.* |

# The Dark Forest

| Dice Roll | Dark Forest – Cliff Face |
|---|---|
| 1 | While climbing down the cliff, you fall part of the way. You hurt your leg. You need to rest. *Lose a turn.* |
| 2-3 | You get stuck halfway down. Stay where you are. *Don't move this turn.* |
| 4-6 | You're a skilful climber and quickly climb down the cliff face. *Next turn swim in the river.* |

# The Mountain Pass

| Dice Roll | Mountain Pass – Landslide |
|---|---|
| Half light half dark stone | You narrowly miss being buried in a landslide. *Go back 2 spaces.* |

# The Mountain Pass

| Dice Roll | Mountain Pass – Great Eagle |
|---|---|
| 1 | The eagle spots you and attacks. You run for your life. *Go back 3 spaces.* |
| 2-3 | The eagle attacks you. You fight it off with your spear but are exhausted. You need to rest. *Lose a turn.* |
| 4-6 | The eagle flies over you but doesn't spot you. You trot forward warily. *Continue on your way.* |

# The Mountain Pass

| Dice Roll | Mountain Pass – Cliff Face |
|---|---|
| 1 | While climbing down the cliff, you fall part of the way. You hurt your leg. You need to rest. *Lose a turn.* |
| 2-3 | You get stuck halfway down. Stay where you are. *Don't move this turn.* |
| 4-6 | You're a skilful climber and quickly climb down the cliff face. *Next turn, swim in the river.* |

## The River Crossing

| Dice Roll | The River Crossing |
|---|---|
| 1 | When attempting to cross the slippery rocks, you fall in the water. *Lose a turn.* |
| 2-3 | You can't cross the river as the water is too high and the current is too strong. *Stay where you are.* |
| 4-6 | You cross successfully. *Next turn consult the mammoth chart.* |

## The Mammoth

| Dice Roll | The Mammoth |
|---|---|
| 1 | The mammoth sees you and charges. You run for your life, back to the safety of the river. *Next turn consult the river crossing chart.* |
| 2-3 | You crouch low in the bushes as the mammoth sniffs the air above you, trying to find you! *Don't move this turn.* |
| 4-6 | The mammoth is distracted by a log you toss to its side. It wanders off to investigate. You sneak past the mammoth. *Next turn consult the terror bird chart.* |

# The Terror Bird

| Dice Roll | The Terror Bird |
|---|---|
| 1 | The terror bird attacks you. Run for your life! You run all the way to the river. Next turn consult the river crossing chart. |
| 2-3 | The terror bird attacks you. You bravely, or foolishly, fend off the terror bird with your spear. Don't move this turn. |
| 4-6 | You take a chance. While the terror bird has its back to you, you run swiftly to the camp. With a loud squawk, the terror bird chases you, but you have a small lead. You *just* make it to the safety of the camp before the terror bird can bite you with its massive beak. **You've made it!** |

# Story Retell

After students have played the game several times, encourage them to narrate what happened in the game. That is, the students *retell* the events of the game. The *Journey Home* game tells a story. Many things can and do happen to the characters. Encourage students to retell what happened to *his/her* particular character.

The events of the game will be different for each player. That is because variation and detail has been built into each scene.

Fortunately, it is not difficult for children to narrate the events of the game. The experience of playing a fun competitive game will still be fresh in each child's memory. Even with a simple oral retell, encourage students to build into their retells a clear *beginning*, *middle* and *end*.

# Story Retell - Sequence

The **beginning** introduces…

- *Who* the main character is
- *What* is the first thing that happens
- *Where* the story takes place
- *When* the story takes place

The **middle** contains…

- The events of the story
- What happened first
- What happened next, etc

The **end** contains…

- How the story ends/story resolution

# Story Retell Example

The following is a verbal retell of the game's events by a 10 year old student.

**Beginning:** "Guff went down the river but he had to wait because the raft was broken. He fixed it and then went down the river. But he went slowly because the river was so slow."

**Middle:** "Guff's raft hit a rock and he got stuck, but then he was moving again. Guff's raft went over a waterfall and he went over with it. Oh no! He landed in the water and swallowed water. He got out of the water and rested."

**Middle:** "Guff floated down the raging river and crossed the river on some rocks. He then had to hide in some bushes from a mammoth. The mammoth tried to find him but Guff was clever and he got away."

**Middle:** "And then Guff had to fight the terror bird, which was a big bird with a big beak. Guff stabbed at the terror bird with his spear."

**End:** "Guff beat the terror bird and made it the camp. He was safe."

# Story Writing Sequence

- When students have played the game a few times and have completed a retell it is time to write down the events of the game onto paper. Writing down the events of the game is like producing a first draft of a story. The goal at this point is just to write down a few events and words.

Use the **Story Grammar Graphic Organizers** to write down the sequence of events the student's character went through. This includes coming up for a *title* for their story, writing down the *initiating event,* the *problem* that the character had to solve and what happened at the end, and the character's *response* to the events in the story. Write a rough draft of the story onto fresh paper.

- Consult the **character profiles** for the main characters and creatures depicted. Each character profile has a range of **nouns**, **verbs** and **adjectives** to assist students to construct sentences with added punch and interesting language.

- Consult the setting profiles for the **Raging River** the **Dark Forest** and the **Mountain Pass**. The setting profiles contain **nouns** and **adjectives** that can be used to add extra colour and variety to your students' written narratives. There is no mention in the game of emotional responses of Guff and Asa to the events on their journey. The students can consult the **emotions chart** to select their character's possible response to an exciting or frightening event.

- Once the story has been written down, encourage students to revise their writing. The best writers constantly revise their written work. Students are to look for spelling and punctuation errors.

- When students have completed their stories promote the idea of using a thesaurus to find synonyms for the words they have used. For example, if a student had written, "Guff *lay* low in the bushes," this could be changed to "Guff crouched low in the bushes, "etc.

- Once students have gained some confidence from writing a story based on the story's events encourage them to play the game again and write another story. The game has many varied possible events to explore.

- When students have written a few stories based on the game, they will have a reasonable grasp of story writing rules and will be better able to imagine and construct their *own* stories.

# Story Sequence Example

What follows is an example of a completed story, which includes all the steps required to create the story, obtained from the individual parts of the program. The sequence can be broken down into several steps. The completed story was constructed and written by 10 year old student, Daniel.

**Step 1**: Daniel played the *Journey Home* board game and made a note of all the events that took place. His character, Guff, took the *Dark Forest* route. He encountered the fierce *saber-toothed cat* and had to run into the bushes to survive. He eventually evaded the cat and was able to make it to the cliff face. While climbing down the *cliff face* Guff gets stuck halfway and then falls to the ground. He hurts his leg and has to rest.

After resting, Guff swims down the *Raging River*, crosses the river over rocks and hides from the *mammoth*. The mammoth discovers Guff and charges. Guff runs to the safety of the raging river. He crosses the river again and is able to evade the mammoth this time by distracting it. He runs past the *terror bird*. The ferocious bird chases Guff, but Guff has a small lead and makes it to the safety of village before the terror bird can reach him.

**Step 2**: Daniel is encouraged by the clinician to write down the events of the game onto the *Sequence of Events* pages. The goal at this point was for Daniel to jot down notes only. Daniel does this while encouraged by the clinician to verbally retell the events of the story. The verbal retell assists Daniel to remember key events in the game.

**Step 3**: The clinician gives a brief explanation of the *Story Grammar Map* to Daniel. For instance, the *initiating event*, the character's *plans* and *internal response* are discussed. This particular area of story writing may need extensive scaffolding. Understanding story grammar principles is the key to your students being able to effectively write stories. Daniel, with the assistance of the clinician, writes the key events of the game's dramas into the story grammar map boxes.

**Step 4**: Daniel, using the completed story grammar map as a guide, writes a rough draft of the story. He is prompted by the clinician to consult the character profiles charts to help him construct the sentences. Each main character in the game has a number of *nouns*, *verbs* and *adjectives* that can be used by students to add colour and variety to their written description of events.

**Step 5**: Daniel completes his story and titles it *Guff and the Dark Forest*. Daniel is encouraged by the clinician to carefully reread the story several times and correct any spelling and punctuation errors. After completing the first story, Daniel has an increased confidence in story writing. He plays the game again and discovers that the events this time, due to the randomness of the dice, are quite different. It gives him enough information for another story. Daniel is encouraged to add extra colour and detail to his new story. In time, Daniel will have the tools and the confidence to independently construct his own stories.

# Daniel's Story

## Guff and the Dark Forest

Guff is a Neanderthal boy. He has a spear and wears clothes made from a bear skin. One day Guff gets lost and has to go home to his village through the dark forest. He walks down the green track and a saber-toothed cat sees him. Guff runs for his life. He is terrified. The cat chases Guff but Guff hides in the bushes. Guff then walks down the track again and walks past lots of vines and big green leaves.

Guff sees a cliff and has to climb down it. He falls and hurts his leg. He says ouch and has to rest until his leg gets better. He then swims in the river which takes him all the way to a river crossing. He gets out of the water and crosses the river on big rocks. Oh no, he sees a mammoth. The mammoth is huge and enormous. The mammoth attacks Guff and he runs back to the river where it is safe. Guff throws a stick behind the mammoth and the mammoth goes to look for it. Guff runs past the mammoth and it doesn't see him.

Guff runs past the terror bird. The terror bird is really ferocious and fast. It chases Guff but Guff is faster. He makes it to the camp and is safe. Guff is excited and happy to be home.

# Character Profiles

**Guff** is a boy who lives in prehistoric times. He has been out hunting for rabbits and has become lost, a long way from his village. Guff wears clothes made from wolf and bear skin.

**Asa** is Guff's sister. Asa has been fishing in a fast flowing river and was chased by a large saber-toothed cat. She has now become separated from her tribe. She must find her way back home.

# Character Profiles

## Character Profiles

### Character: Guff

Words to assist story writing

Description: Guff is a teenage boy who wears clothes made from bearskins and fox fur. He is stocky, strong, and carries a spear.

Words to describe Guff

Noun: spear, handle, hair, rug, skill, boots, his, he.

Verbs: run, running, swim, swam, walk, walked, hid, hide, climbed, dive, dived, dove, thrust, defended, hearing heard, froze, rest, crouch, crouched

Adjective: strong, powerful, tired, exhausted, confused, weary, frightened, brave, bravely, daring, bold, confident

Adverbs: slowly, quickly, carelessly, carefully

never, soon, later

Example: Guff bravely **dove** into the river as the raft over the waterfall.

### Character: Asa

Words to assist story writing

Description: Asa is a young girl who wears clothes made from bearskins and fox fur. She is small, slim and very brave.

Words to describe Asa

Nouns:, hair, rug, skill, boots, basket, fishing line, her, she.

Verbs: run, running, swim, swam, walk, walked, hid, hide, climbed, dive, dived, dove, thrust, defended, hearing, heard, froze, rest. crouch, crouched.

Adjective: strong, ducked, tired, confused, weary, frightened, brave, bravely, daring, bold, confident, quick, fast, tiny.

Adverbs: slowly, quickly, carelessly, carefully, never, soon, later.

Example: Asa ***heard*** the cat ***walking*** through the forest. ***She quickly climbed*** a tree to escape the fierce predator.

# Character Profiles

| | |
|---|---|
| **Character:** Saber-Toothed Cat | **Verbs:** ran, charge, charged, hunted, hunt, stalked, walked, stood, rested, tear, sprint, sprinted, roar, roared, growled<br><br>**Adjective:** ferocious, fierce, dangerous, huge, enormous, cunning, menacing, fast, faster, attack, sniff, sniffed.<br><br>**Adverb:** quickly, slowly, quietly, silently |
| **Words to assist story writing**<br><br>**Description:** Saber-toothed cats were ferocious predators that lived in pre-historic times. They had enormous tearing teeth on their upper jaw.<br><br>**Words to describe the saber-toothed cat**<br><br>**Noun:** cat, cat, predator, hunter, animal, teeth, fur, tail. | **Example:** The ***ferocious*** saber-toothed cat ***sprinted*** after Asa. Asa quickly climbed a tree. |
| **Character:** Mammoth | **Verbs:** walked, ran, charged, stood, standing, roar, roared, trumpet, trumpeted, thundered, sniff, sniffed, strode<br><br>**Adjective:** enormous, big, great, strength, mighty, power, majestic, attacks, aggressive, rush, wooly, hairy.<br><br>**Adverbs:** slowly, menacingly, loudly, noisily |
| **Words to assist story writing**<br><br>**Description:** The wooly mammoth was a prehistoric type of elephant. It was covered in long hair, had small ears, and featured long curved tusks.<br><br>**Words to describe the mammoth**<br><br>**Nouns:** hair, tusks, trunk, ears, hooves, tail. | **Example:** The ***great*** mammoth **strode** over to where Guff hid in the bushes. It ***sniffed*** the air ***menacingly*** above where Guff crouched. |

# Character Profiles

| Character: Haast Eagle | Verbs: swooped, flew, soared, hovered, glide, drifted, dived, attacked.<br>Adjectives: majestic, massive, striking, afraid, fearing, fear, risky, unprotected.<br>Adverbs: quietly, silently, quickly, swiftly |
|---|---|
| **Words to assist story writing**<br>Description: The Great Eagle became extinct about 1500 C.E. The Haast eagle was much larger than a modern eagle. A modern eagle weighs about 5 kg's whereas a Haast eagle weighed 15 kg's.<br>**Words to describe the Great Eagle**<br>Nouns: eagle, feathers, talons, beak, wing | Example: The **massive** eagle **swooped** down **swiftly.** Guff covered his **unprotected** head with his spear. The eagle **glided** briefly and then **soared** high into the sky. |
| Character: Terror Bird | Verbs: walked, ran, run, bolted, charged, attacked, hide hid, sprint, sprinted, hunted, squawked, pursued.<br>Adjective: ferocious, fierce, dangerous, huge, enormous, cunning, menacing, fast, faster, massive.<br>Adverbs: quietly, silently, quickly, swiftly. |
| **Words to assist story writing**<br>Description: The terror bird was a large, carnivorous flightless bird. The terror bird was about 8-10 feet high and ferocious.<br>**Words to describe the Terror Bird**<br>Nouns: beak, feathers, claws, predator | Example: Asa tried to sneak past the terror bird, but the **massive predator** heard her. With a loud **squawk** it **pursued** Asa. |

# Setting Profiles

## **Setting:** The Dark Forest

**Words to assist story writing**

Description: The dark forest is a place full of trees and bushes. It's hard to see anything, even two feet in front of you.

**Words to describe the Dark Forest**

Nouns: flora, vegetation, bloom, bush, scrub, trees, vines, branch, trunk, leaves, swamp, shade, hot.

Adjectives: overgrown, lush, flowering, leafy, weedy.

## **Setting:** The Mountain Pass

**Words to assist story writing**

Description: The mountain pass is a treacherous place. The mountains are beautiful, cold and dangerous. Landslides are common here.

**Words to describe the Mountain Pass**

Nouns: high altitude, summit, mount, mountain, range, hill, rocks, rocky landslide, peak.

Adjectives: soaring, towering, lofty.

## **Setting:** The Raging River

**Words to assist story writing**

Description: The Raging River is a dangerous waterway that leads to a towering waterfall.

**Words to describe the Raging River**

Nouns: water, waterfall, falls, spring, fountain, current, eddy, whirlpool, rapids, cascade, force.

Adjectives: flowing, winding

Example: (Dark Forest) Asa walked along the path through the **lush vegetation** of the dark forest. Suddenly, she stopped. In front of her was a saber tooth cat. She hid behind a **flowering bush**.

Example: (Raging River) Guff rode the raft over the **rapids**. He dove into the **water** as it **cascaded** over the **falls**.

Example: (Mountain Pass) Asa climbed the **rocks** to the top of the **mountain peak**. She looked at the **towering mountains** that surrounded her.

# Story Map

**Story Title**

**Setting**: Where is the story set?

**Story Start**: What problem sets the story in motion?

**Internal response**: What does the character feel?

**Plan**: What does the character plan to do?

**Attempts**: What does the character do about the problem?

1

2

3

**Resolution**: What happens at the end? How does the character feel at the end of the story?

# Story Map *Example*

**Story Title**

*Guff and the Dark Forest*

Setting: Where is the story set?

*In the dark forest, and in the prehistoric world.*

Story Start: What problem sets the story in motion?

*Guff becomes separated from his tribe and has to travel through the dark forest to find his way home.*

Internal response: What does the character feel?

*Guff is concerned but very brave. The animals he meets are terrifying but he bravely faces them.*

Plan: What does the character plan to do?

*The character decides to go into the dark forest because it will eventually lead him home.*

Attempts: What does the character do about the problem?

1 *He walks through the dark forest.*

2 *He climbs down the cliff and then swims down the Raging River*

3 *He comes across many fierce creatures but cleverly evades them*

Resolution: What happens at the end? How does the character feel at the end of the story?

*Guff is relieved and happy to be alive and proud because he survived the dangers of a harsh world alone.*

# Playing Pieces – Guff and Asa

Photocopy and cut out the playing pieces. Attach the pieces to card or laminate. Two sizes are available - A3 and A4. The board game on page 244 can be resized from A4 to A3 on most photocopiers. *Figures are **Asa** with her fishing pole and **Guff** with his spear.* If more than two players are playing, use different *coloured* paper under the base of each character to identify the character and make up new names as needed.

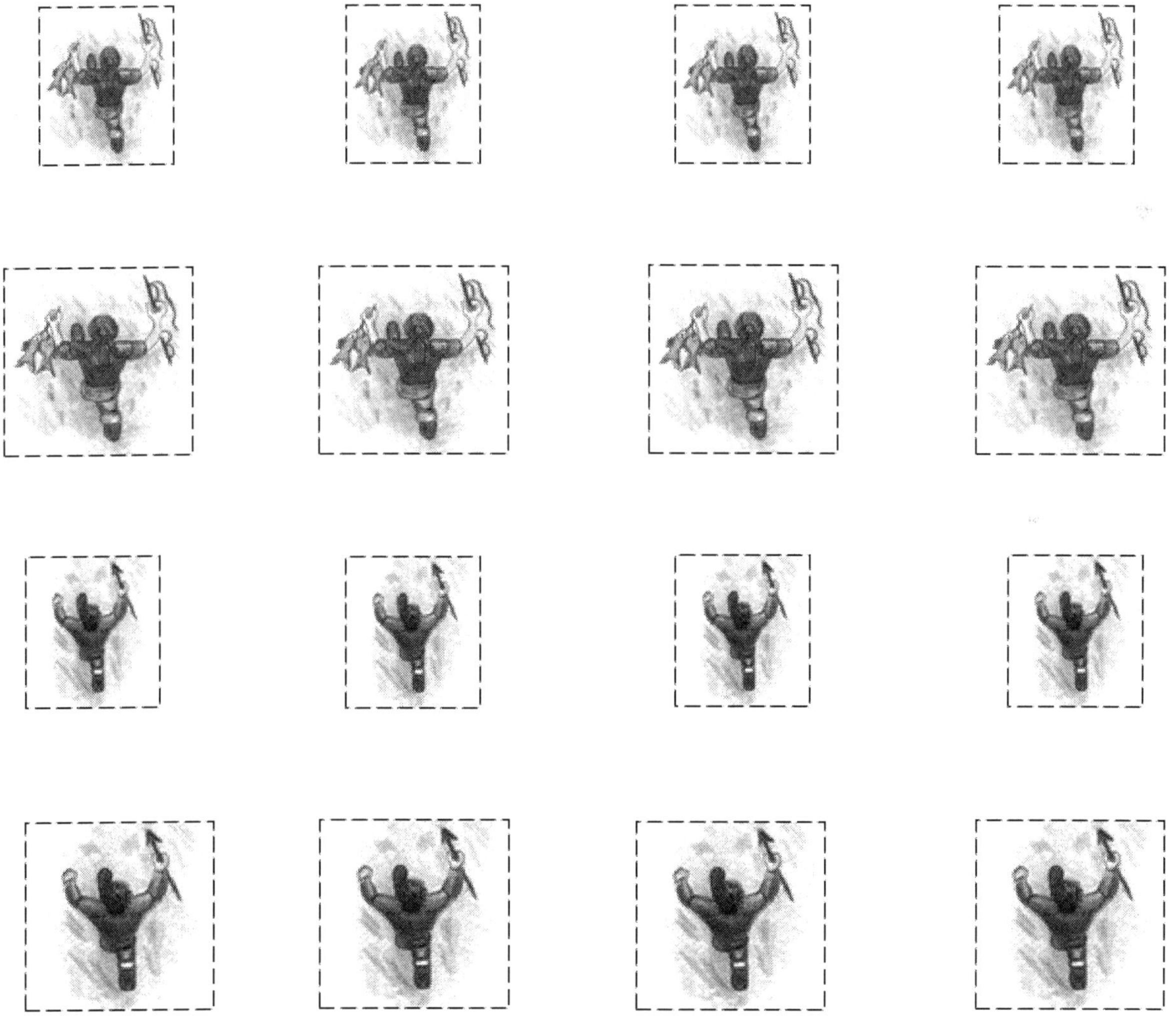

# Playing Pieces – Prehistoric Animals

Photocopy and cut out the playing pieces and either attach to card or laminate for extra durability. The playing pieces can be placed on the game board when the animals are referred to during game play. Instructions for animal placement is on page 225.

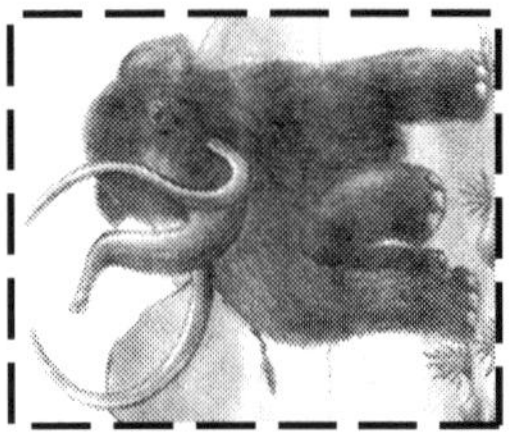
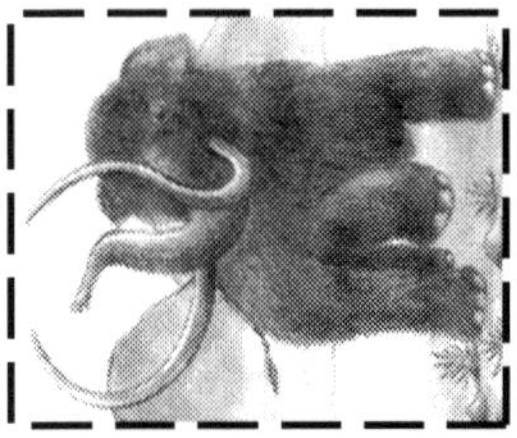

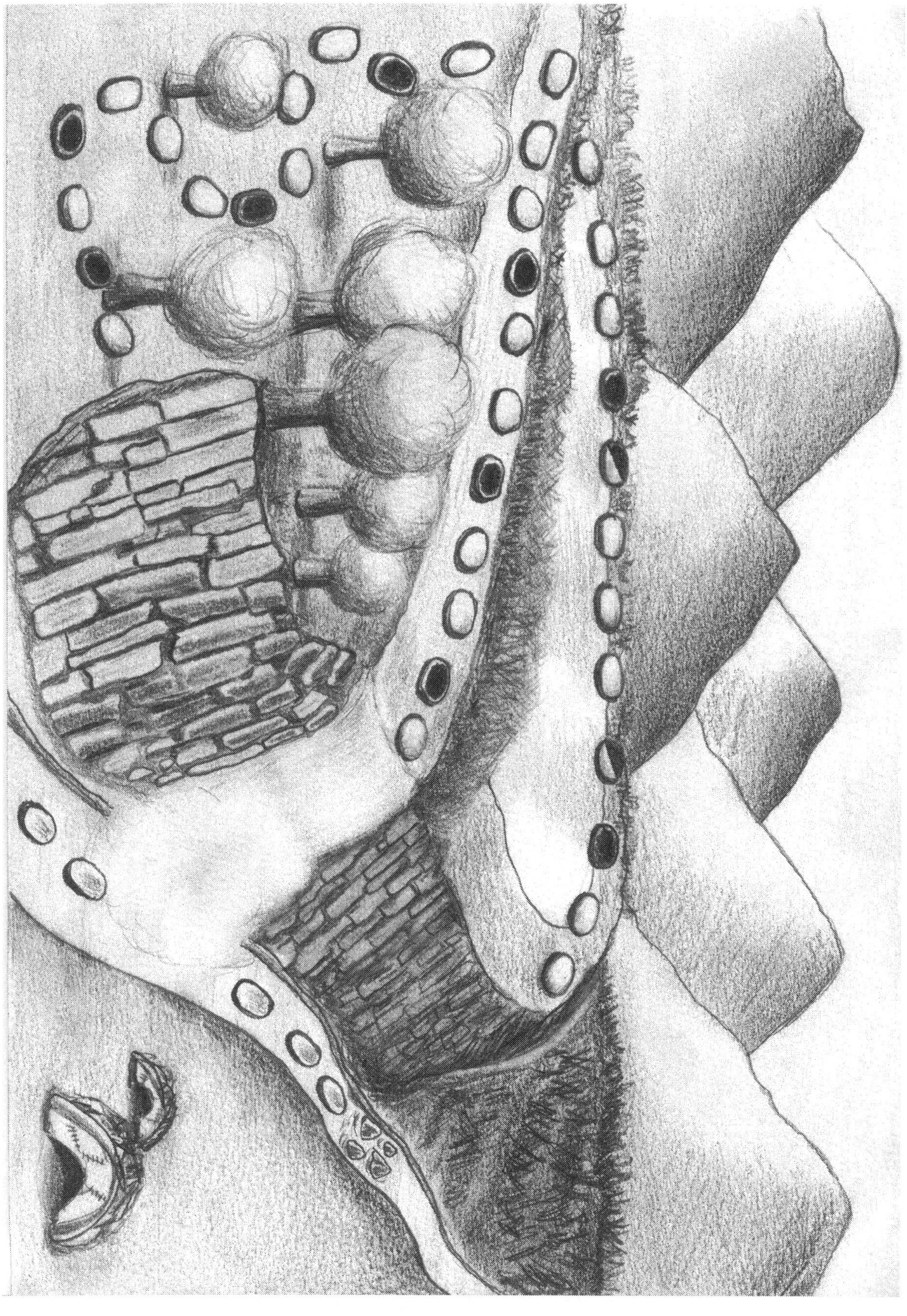

# About the Author

David Newman is speech-language pathologist and writer in his spare time who lives and works in Victoria, Australia.

David self publishes books and workbooks to help school-age children acquire language and literacy skills. Starting from scratch, David's popular website - **speech-language-resources.com** - has hundreds of user-friendly webpages and a wealth of free programs, games and guides to assist teachers, parents and speech-language pathologists improve children's speech, and oral and written language skills.

David is a full-time speech-language pathologist working in Victorian schools. He writes workbooks mostly in his spare time often curled up on the couch cradling a laptop huddled near a gas heater (Colac is *frosty* in the winter) sipping cups of hot tea or playing with his young son.

If you found this book helpful or valuable, please let me know by posting a positive **review** for it on **Amazon.com**.

**www.speechlanguage-resources.com**

David can be contacted via email: **newman.david.j@edumail.vic.gov.au**

21096676R00139

Printed in Great Britain
by Amazon